Breakfast Epiphanies

Breakfast Epiphanies

Finding Wonder in the Everyday

🌀

DAVID ANDERSON

BEACON PRESS   Boston

Beacon Press
25 Beacon Street
Boston, Massachusetts 02108-2892
www.beacon.org

Beacon Press books
are published under the auspices of
the Unitarian Universalist Association of Congregations.

Printed in the United States of America
06 05 04 03 02   8 7 6 5 4 3 2 1

This book is printed on acid-free paper that meets
the uncoated paper ANSI/NISO specifications
for permanence as revised in 1992.

Text design by Melodie Wertelet
Composition by Wilsted & Taylor Publishing Services

Library of Congress Cataloging-in-Publication Data

Anderson, David.
Breakfast epiphanies : finding wonder in the everyday / David Anderson.
p. cm.
ISBN 0-8070-2818-5 (alk. paper)
1. Spiritual life — Christianity. 2. Christian life — Anecdotes. I. Title.
BV4501.3 .A52 2002
242 — dc21
2002006176

To
the people of Trinity Church
Solebury, Pennsylvania

Contents

Contents

◎ *Mysteries — Large and Small*

Introduction

Several years ago I ran into a friend at a dinner party. When I asked him how he was doing, he told me he'd had a tough day. "My car stalled on I-95 just out of town," he said, "and I had to wait an hour for a tow truck."

Suddenly a scene flashed on my eye. "Oh," I said, "that was *you* — in the blue car? I was out there today and drove right past. I didn't really look — I just saw a car and someone standing there. If I'd known it was you, I would've stopped!"

That pretty much sums up my search for God: If I'd known it was You, I would've stopped.

This little book is about the times I was lucky enough to stop. Usually I don't, even though I'm a pastor. I'm too busy. My mind is on more immediate things, like *Can I make it to the bank, the car wash, the cleaners, and still make two hospital visits this afternoon?* But every so often it happens. The blinders slip for a moment and I see that my humdrum life is somehow implicated in the Big Big Picture. There is in fact some ultimate purpose in this drama, and I have a speaking part. These epiphanies are not always glorious; there are moments when I understand how pain has a strangely rightful place, and how inscrutable life finally is. But even then, it is enough to know that this is the truth.

The stories I tell are the ones I've lived. I'm married with two kids. For ten years I've been writing about faith and life, first for the newsletter of the Episcopal church where I serve as rector, and then for the newspaper of the Episcopal Diocese of Pennsylvania. Most of the pieces in this book were written first for the people I live and work with. I decided from the start never to write about church and never to use churchly language. I wanted to talk about what was happening in my own experience — where God was turning up unexpectedly, and where, frankly, he wasn't.

As a pastor I hear constant complaints that life is too busy, too routinized. Stress is enemy number one. So I skip the big topics and write about everyday things, like cleaning up after a storm, waiting in the doctor's office, or fighting a traffic ticket. If we can't find God here, what good is "spirituality"?

Since we are formed and shaped mostly by our relationships, I write about sharing dinner-party preparations with my wife, and about family arguments in our house that turn ugly. I chronicle a harrowing trip to the dress shop with my two adolescent daughters, and a beautifully awkward and triumphant date to my first father-daughter dance. I talk about the death of my mother and the trip home to visit my widowed father. Somehow in these ordinary moments I believe we are susceptible to a new, sometimes offbeat awareness of the divine presence.

Besides struggling to find meaning and direction in my own life and in the intimate life of my family, I work every day as a pastor, listening to the lives of seven hundred parishioners. I've been drinking coffee and sharing stories, counseling, praying, and making midnight hospital calls here for ten years. So I tell the stories of our life together. I write about the death of a five-year-old boy, about the buzz I got at a service of healing, about a final blessing for eight children. And I remember the night we watched our church burn down, and how we crawled out of the rubble and back to life again.

I hope you enjoy these stories. And I hope they suggest a new way of seeing the world that uncovers transcendence in the ordinary. I keep hoping that if I tell enough of these stories I'll see the next one coming a mile away and I'll pull off the road and say, "I thought it might be You, so I stopped."

I wish that for you, too.

Family
Affairs

🌀

Breakfast Epiphanies

This morning our family of four had cereal and bile for breakfast. Here, in the typically random order of family feuds, was the menu:

- Who had not changed the kitty litter
- Who had not cleaned her room
- Who had not practiced the piano
- Who had not participated — *happily* — in the family yard-work project
- And, of course, whose attitude stunk

Actually that is only what my wife and I were serving up from our side of the table. On the other side, our thirteen- and fifteen-year-old daughters were slinging a mean hash of their own.

- Who could not stop harassing innocent children
- Who had always favored the other child
- Who needed serious therapy for dirty laundry fixation

Things got louder and a cereal box was slammed on the table. One daughter retreated into an eye-rolling "I give up on this family." The other ejected herself from the room. Mercifully, our weekday breakfast is only an eight-minute affair and no one was injured because the bus came, as usual, at 7:10.

We did not stand at the door and kiss them good-bye as we always do. We sat at the table and they left in contempt without closing the door behind them.

I took a bitter sip of coffee and felt like a toad. (I was the cereal slammer.) I could not even commiserate with my wife. The night before I had insisted it was time for one of our famous family conferences where the law would be laid down. Pam had agreed things were out of control, but, she suggested, that likely was because *we* were not in control. I had been preoccupied with church work, she reminded me, and out of town a lot; she had been preoccupied with her business and gone more than usual. If we wanted the kids to get back on track, she said, we'd better get our priorities back in line. We were the parents. We had to restore some calm to the family system and not make the kids the "problem."

I sighed heavily. "I love how you've analyzed the situation," I said, "to the point where these kids aren't accountable and it's really our fault." I got up and left with a hugely passive-aggressive shrug. "Fine," I said, "then we'll do nothing. Have it your way."

But there I sat, having provoked my family conference anyway. I heard an echo of my own words a moment earlier. In the middle of that pitched argument, our older daughter had come to tears and I had said, "Oh, that's great — just burst into tears when you don't have anything else to say for yourself. I wish I could just cry like that!" Maybe I spoke truer than I knew.

I hate it when I have to admit that, despite my righteous indignation, I am part of the problem. I like my anger clean and simple. If my kids are out of line, I want them to shape up. I don't want to fool with the bigger picture because, of course, that is the picture I show up in. I am part of a whole generation of largely boomer parents who want the privileges and joys of parenthood — namely, children who grow beautifully into adolescence and beyond — without taking the difficult responsibilities of being an adult.

We all want our children to shape up without first looking at the shape of our own lives. We want them to pitch in and take their part in the life of the family, even though we're almost never home. We want them to stay free of drugs and alcohol, when they can see what dominates our adult parties. We stand back, bewildered by the young adults our children are becoming, when we have not taken the time to know them and to guide them, when we have not had the courage to set the boundaries and make the demands that authenticate love. In our frustration we careen wildly between rash punishment and abdication.

Something better requires self-examination and, more, an actual willingness to change. If we love our kids enough to say, "No, you're not going there tonight," it means that we must be prepared to stay home and help make something better happen. It's just easier to complain in hackneyed terms about "kids these days," as we head out the door for the evening we had planned.

It takes inner, adult-style maturity to look within ourselves and ask, "How am I contributing to this problem?" — in our families and in our communities. We live more and more in a culture of spiritual immaturity that teaches us to say, "We have a problem and you must change!"

I left breakfast and went to work, where I promptly rearranged my day's calendar. "3:30 — Be home when kids arrive," I wrote. If I needed to make some changes and give these kids my time, I'd better start today.

I met them at the door, reclaimed the morning's lost kiss, and said, "Sorry about breakfast." My fifteen-year-old tucked the apology in her pocket and said with an impish smile, "Don't worry about it, Dad. You're so obnoxious we don't even listen anymore."

My heart leapt up. Everything was back to normal.

Grace on the Rack

I have been asked as a father to do many things with my two daughters. So when my wife asked me to take the girls dress shopping for new fall dresses, I innocently agreed. How bad could it be?

Actually, my girls weren't girls anymore — Maggie was thirteen and Sharon was eleven — and my failure to comprehend this was the root of all suffering. As we riffled through the first rack of fall offerings, Sharon paused to observe, "Dad, you've never taken us dress shopping, Mom always does. It feels . . . funny." I arched my eyebrows and she quickly added, " — But nice. I like it." I mistakenly took this as a compliment.

My second mistake was to make a suggestion. I held up a pretty print dress for Maggie's opinion. Her eyes raked the dress disdainfully, as if I had held up a dead animal, and she moved toward the dresses laden with zippers and chains. Meanwhile, a young salesclerk whisked Sharon off to look for the perfect dress with a glance that said, "Let's get away from your silly old father. I know the *perfect* look for you!" I held up my hand and tried to call out, "Wait — I know she looks older, but she's only eleven." They were gone.

My third mistake was like unto the second. (It was late; I'm a slow learner.) Maggie held up for my approval a sea foam green, double-knit thing that I mistook for a women's league bowling shirt. She was hurt, convinced I delighted in cruelty, when in fact I just didn't get it.

By the third store my legs had given out and I found myself sitting sheepishly in a chair by the dressing rooms. (Why aren't women this uncomfortable in men's stores?) I watched my daughters in a revolving procession that careened from gaudy to glory (whatever I thought was glorious, of course, was not). Whenever judgment was called for, all the saleswomen agreed with my daughters and smiled at me with either pitied amusement or condescension.

At the end of the day, however, we had two dresses in the bag. Dresses they liked and I had learned to like. I don't know how it happened exactly. I did most everything wrong and everybody came home happy. Which, as I think of it, isn't a bad example of grace. I now know that, at least when it comes to daughters and dresses, grace happens when you hit the stores. Just being there counts for everything. How well you do hardly matters.

A Party to Dinner

I married my wife for her pluck. Pam tells it straight. She is full of grace — and truth. And woe to he (meaning mostly: me) who is lulled by that grace and forgets the truth. It will hit him like a haymaker.

It smacked me, for example, one Saturday when we were giving a dinner party. I spent the morning at church preparing a gaggle of crying babies, parents, and god-parents for baptism. I also stopped by my office — just to check my messages. (I don't know why, but this can take hours.)

About one-ish I walked in the front door. When Pam looked up at me from the beans she was snapping, I could tell I had stayed too long at the office. Nevertheless, I smiled as if to say, Well, isn't this all lovely? The crooked smile that slewed my way said, Don't push it, buddy.

Nothing if not perceptive, I ditched my briefcase, changed clothes, and presented myself for duty. I put a few things in the dishwasher, and then stood there. It was plenty awkward. Finally I heard myself say: "Well, what do you want me to do?" As soon as it escaped my lips I could not believe my own innocent stupidity. I might as well have said, "It would be hard, darling, to care any less about this party, but there you are."

Wiping her hands on a towel, she said in quiet anger,

"I don't want to *tell* you what to do. You're smart enough to figure out what needs to be done and do it! This isn't *my* party — you're not 'helping' me. This is *our* party — we're doing this together, and I simply want you to act like you have a stake here."

I knew what to do. The house must be picked up, the front step swept, the table set, the red sauce simmered. Someone must go for candles, for wine, for two tomatoes and chicken stock. So why do I want to be told what to do?

Beyond simple perversity and selfishness (I want the fun of the party, but I don't want to be put out), it all comes down to the work of a relationship. Relationships are hard, and especially hard for men. We know this. Even the beer commercials now ironically poke fun at this male difficulty.

Entering into a mature relationship — and marriage is the greatest, most common — entails daunting risks. I will be invited into the darkness and light of the other's body and soul, and as W. H. Auden put it, I "will see rare beasts and have unique adventures." But I will also be asked to change and endure the pain of growth. My sin will be made manifest, as will the sin of my spouse, and we will both have to accept and forgive and go on. I need not be terribly successful at all of this. I am only required every day to be faithful, to come to the table.

The opposite of this, if you must be reminded, is to come home late in the middle of preparations for a shared dinner party and ask for your marching orders like a hired hand who just punched the clock.

Just tell me what to do. I am always mystified, when

men talk among themselves, how proud they are to be lackeys at home. How openly they discuss the servile ways in which they report to "the boss." Often these are men who manage people by the score and budgets by the million.

As a parish pastor I see men who "rule the world" come into church and sit down. Some of them, their whole bodies change. Shoulders slacken and their genuine authority seems to puddle in their socks. They're not in their element. Something inner, spiritual, emotional is being demanded, and they don't know what to do. When they come up against the demands of a love relationship with God, they often stammer, "Just tell me what to do, Reverend." I want to say, "If you were about to dance with a woman, would you walk onto the floor and say, 'Just tell me what to do'?"

One can hardly speak about the progress of a marriage without segueing into the progress of the soul. No other experience lies closer to the heart of our spiritual lives than marriage — or any lifelong union. In trying to image the union of God and humanity, the Hebrew Scriptures and the New Testament both repeatedly reach for the metaphor of marriage. If we want to practice the disciplines and habits that make for union with God, we are told to start with our spouse. What we learn in one relationship informs the other; the traffic goes both ways, from earth to heaven.

And so it is not a long ways from our dinner party to the divine. God will not tell us what to do any more than my wife would. (There are many sects and churches that are only too happy to oblige anyone who wants to be told what to do. They will even threaten you with damnation for failure if it makes you feel any better. But if this is beneath even my wife, surely it is unworthy of God.) We already know what to do if we are to live as one. Come to the table. Open ourselves both to bliss and risk. Commit ourselves to this thing as if we have a stake.

On this point, count yourself lucky (I do) if you live with someone who "won't take any *merde*," as the French would say it. Someone who can smell the stuff a mile away and call it cold. Someone who will press you and push you, who will not do your work for you. A person who can get angry about one thing at a time and not use the moment of anger to also name your other faults but, rather, simply stand there and insist that you live as one, now, in the midst of preparing for this simple dinner party, and in every other moment of your shared life together, world without end.

Dance for the Other

I have mostly bad memories of my dating days. I had all the usual problems, from acne to zero self-confidence. So why am I so pleased to be putting on this suit and picking up a corsage for my newest date?

For starters, I didn't have to screw up my courage and pick up the phone. The invitation to the annual Father-Daughter Dance arrived in the mail, and she came waltzing into my office saying, "It's us — let's go!" I like this already.

We arrive at the banquet hall, check our coats, and begin mingling. There are little girls in pinafores and big bows; older girls I've only seen in school uniforms or soccer jerseys who seem beautifully, uncomfortably overdressed; seniors who carry themselves with grace beyond their slender years. Dress-up events like this present us fathers with clear evidence to support our one hope and fear: these girls are turning into women before our eyes.

The girls hit us up for soda money and disappear into their regular circles of friends. This is much like a pre-adolescent group date, where all the girls cluster happily together and leave the hapless boys alone to wonder what this is all about. Left alone, the fathers get something a little stronger at the bar. We talk about sports, politics, and school business while we keep an eye on our girls. One nine- or ten-year-old comes racing over, sliding the last three feet on the slick soles of her patent leather shoes. "Here," she says, thrusting a beautiful satin jacket at her father. "Mom made me wear this and I hate it — it's hot." A young woman, pocketless in her spaghetti-strap dress, coolly asks her father to hold her lipstick.

We do not mention our feelings at this moment. The most we do is smile and shake our heads and shrug a little. We are so proud it is killing us, and every man is thinking of exactly the same thing. We are all envisioning a wedding (and worrying about a lot of dates between now and then). We cannot believe how quickly this all happens, how a dozen years can fly by, and how in a dozen more we could be all tuxed up and walking these children down the aisle. Quietly we are doing the math in our heads, while "Sunrise, Sunset," the wedding song from *Fiddler on the Roof*, is playing in our ears.

Meanwhile we shell out more money for sodas and complain that our wives are getting the night off.

Soon we are called to the dining room. When I pull out the chair to seat my thirteen-year-old, she glances at me with a furtive, surprised smile: this is new, slightly embarrassing in front of all her friends — my treating her like a royal. Not bad for me either. This social ritual can't help but remind me of my own gawky, angst-ridden dating days. Trying to appear composed and worldly, trying to impress. But tonight it's all about this girl — making this night perfect for her.

After picking at the chicken à la king, we go to have our picture taken. The man behind the camera tells us we are a handsome couple, and when we get the Polaroid back in the paper frame, we agree.

By the time we get back to dinner, the littlest girls are already skipping and twirling on the dance floor. They plead with the DJ to start the music and he does. And then it is our turn. The fathers. I place my napkin on the table, clear my throat, and ask her to dance. Again that smile.

I am not a good dancer at all. I think too much and forget the steps; I keep looking at other, better dancers; I feel self-conscious and cannot abandon myself to music and movement together. But this does not matter tonight. You can dance like the wind, I discover, when your only hope is to turn every tentative, little girl's step into a thing of beauty. Why am I surprised that freedom and fulfillment come the moment we stop thinking about ourselves and live for something beyond?

Driving home I let her choose the radio station without the usual fight. We hold hands. I know this will be gone in the morning, when the regular tug-of-war between teen and parents resume. But this is good. All my little failures as a father, all my crazy frustration at trying to be a decent man, are somehow redeemed in this moment. I can spend whole afternoons wondering if I have broken the first charge of the father's Hippocratic oath, "First do no harm." And then in one, self-evaporating whirl around the floor I know what I am here for. Dance for the Other.

Ripley's in the Rain

What do you do on a family vacation when it rains? A few summers ago when rains drove us from the beach, we spent whole days going duckpin bowling, shopping for little gewgaws, and watching a boy in a candy shop make saltwater taffy. It was bleak. But with kids, you've got to do something.

It rained again on a recent vacation, and that, as I'm about to tell you, is how I ended up at the Ripley's "Believe It or Not!" Museum in Gatlinburg, Tennessee. I agreed to take the kids and, to tell you the truth, I could have dropped them off. But I was a little curious, which is what Mr. Ripley understood about people — even nice, law-abiding, churchgoing people like me. We'll pay to see a two-headed goat because, well . . . because it's raining and our lives are so predictable. All our goats are strictly one-headed.

I paid the sucker's price and I saw the (stuffed) two-headed goat advertised on the marquee, as well as a two-faced little calf. It was a little sad, actually. I felt like I had slouched into a tent at the turn of the century to see the bearded lady. There was also a four-legged South American Rhea (a bird). I got down on one knee to see if they had glued on the two extra legs. I couldn't tell.

I saw a black-and-white video of a man who smoked

through his eye. He put the cigarette in his eye and some-how got the smoke to come out his nose. That was a little sad, too. I saw "Butch, the dog who eats glass" and "Vast, the horse that gallops backwards."

Feeling cheapened but determined to redeem the price of admission I pressed on to see genuine shrunken heads, the work of Jivaro Indians in Ecuador, and a lock of hair from the Father of Our Nation. Remember the little paper chains we used to make out of gum wrappers? I saw one 6,583 feet long, woven into a rug by schoolteacher Nicholas Miller of Barnhart, Missouri. How long, you're wondering, did it take Mr. Miller to make the rug? Eighteen years.

By the time I got to the tomb of Santa Claus and the death mask of John Dillinger ("made directly from the face of Dillinger by the local coroner"), I went for some fresh air. It was still raining.

I stood there under an awning watching the crowds and wondering what sorts of lives we were all living. Why would people (present company included) line up in the rain and pay six bucks to see the bizarre, the tasteless, and the kitschy? What, exactly, was I doing at the tomb of Santa Claus?

I felt implicated in some cultural dysfunction, and for a moment I thought seriously about what I ought to do about that. Until I remembered that I was on vacation.

After a while my kids came out and said, "Pretty cool, huh, Dad?" And I said, "Unbelievable."

Graveyard Stew

Sometime in my thirties I started having trouble sleeping. Occasionally I'd lie awake for hours, my mind churning like a computer scanning files at a million bytes a second. I counted sheep; I counted forward and backward, by twos and fives; I imagined being the tiredest I've ever been; I tried emptying my mind. One night, when none of that worked, a curative memory came to me like a revelation.

When my father could not sleep — which was not often — he put on his slippers and headed for the kitchen. One night, as a boy, I heard someone clanking around and padded down to investigate. I found him at the stove, stirring something in an old saucepan. That's the night I was delivered the tradition, the ritual of Graveyard Stew.

If you don't know this simple delicacy, it's basically milk toast. But for my father it was wee-hour comfort food, the only Sominex in the house (my mother barely believed in aspirin). The recipe is simple. My father never actually taught me this, and of course I never saw a recipe written down. I just watched and ate.

Begin with an old saucepan, the oldest, most beat-up and blackened one you've got. Put it on the stove and pour whole milk into it. Medium heat. Get a big old spoon and stir. Back and forth. Back and forth, my father would drag the heavy spoon across the bottom of the pan. (Don't skip the stirring part. The back and forth of the spoon is soothing and hypnotic and helps put you to sleep, which is why you're making this.) Keep stirring. That spoon raking the heavy bottom of the pan sounded to me like chains being dragged across a subterranean tomb. But that could just be the boy trying to understand why they called it Graveyard Stew. I don't know. I just do what my dad did — stir.

When little wisps of steam begin to rise, float a slab of butter on the milk. Keep stirring. As the butter melts, stare at the little golden purls that ripple out behind your spoon. Back and forth. Now drop in a pinch of salt and — my favorite part — a good shower of pepper. Watch the pepper float black on white on streaks of gold.

By now steam should be steadily rising. You want to be just this side of scalding the milk; you don't want to boil it. Best thing is to stick your fingertip into the milk. When you have to yank it right back out, it's ready.

My dad taught me to eat Graveyard Stew right out of the pan. I recommend it, unless you have to share in bowls. I always felt like a cowboy eating out of an old pot by an open fire. You take a box of saltines with you to the table and drop a couple of crackers in the stew. Crunch them up with your big spoon and eat. I don't like soggy crackers, so I only put in a few at a time.

I doubt I shared Graveyard Stew with my father more than three or four times. But that sleepless night it all came back to me. I knew instinctively how to make this milky thing as if I had always done it. But my eyes were only partly opened. The fullness of revelation came when I tasted again the pepper, the butter, and the milk together. It doesn't taste that good, but that's not important.

I don't suppose the young Proust really loved madeleines all that much. (I've had them and they're better than vanilla wafers — but let's leave it at that.) It just happened one winter day that when he tasted a few crumbs of them in his hot tea, a lost piece of his past came magically to life on his palate. That's what happened to me when I tasted the crackers crumbled in hot, peppery milk in a blackened saucepan. Big old spoon in hand, eyes locked open to receive the vision.

It was unmistakably the taste of masculine love. The milk of the father. Midnight intimacy with a strong man who was quiet and not really one to show affection. But he could feed me, take me into the ritual, honor me as a bearer of the tradition.

Memory is funny this way. Suddenly I was given a past: I had that kind of father. So what if I had forgotten it. The experience was coded on my tongue. It all rushed back upon me with a force no photo album or home movie could muster. This came from within; I held it in my own body. (It works the other way, too. A divorced woman told me once that her son had gotten in a fight, been pinned down. And when he looked into the angry, twisted face of the other boy, he saw his long-gone father and was suddenly reliving a father-attack that must never have happened. He cried and cried, she said.)

In the middle of the night not long ago, I felt a hand shaking me out of deep sleep. Our older daughter was standing beside the bed whispering, "I can't sleep." I'm not good at moments like this. "Have you told your mother?" I said. But I was it. I knew this parent drill: you walk the kid upstairs, tuck her in again, give her a stuffed animal, stroke her forehead a few times, and then fall back into bed. This I did. I was hardly back in bed when I heard her coming down the stairs. "Bad dream." I knew I was in for the longer drill.

I got out of bed. Despite the darkness, I felt for something wool in my sock drawer and grabbed my bathrobe. It was time for Graveyard Stew. I loved seeing her eyes when I told her what we were about to eat. I stirred and told her about my father.

She wanted to stir, too, of course. So I let her stir while I dropped in the butter, the salt and finally the floating black pepper. She stirred in circles and the black pepper and the golden butter swirled in a hypnotic vortex. "Good," I said, coaching her. "You've got the stirring down."

We sat at the kitchen table and talked until the bad dream seemed just that. I taught her how to crumble just a few crackers at a time. Before long, the warm milk had worked its soporific magic, and I was tucking her in again. The tradition was safely handed on.

The next morning my younger daughter confronted me: "When do I get to have Graveyard Stew like Maggie?" And it wasn't many nights before I had another little girl beside my bed in the dead hours saying she just couldn't seem to sleep. Bad dreams.

When I came to pass this culinary heirloom to the next

generation, I wondered for the first time whether what my father called Graveyard Stew bore any resemblance to some official, published recipe. (Families sometimes have funny names for odd things.) I got out several old cookbooks, but "Graveyard Stew" was a nonstarter. I looked up "milk toast" and found that you were supposed to put butter and salt on toast and then pour hot milk over it. You could do that. But I wouldn't, even if it tasted better. Because I eat this — as one eats at Passover — to remember. To remember who I am, and whose I am. Because whenever I get out the old blackened saucepan in the middle of the night, he is there. And I guess I want that for my girls. I want to give them a rite that will always make present the love of the father. And help them sleep, too.

The College Tour

Boarding the Amtrak Silver Star, we were pleasantly surprised when the ticket agent directed us to our seats — in business class. Handing us our stubs, he said, "Hold on to these. You're entitled to free beverage service in that car."

My sixteen-year-old daughter led the way to our seats. We chucked our bags in the overhead and settled down for the ride to Providence, Rhode Island, and on to Boston. Armed with *The Fiske Guide to Colleges*, Princeton Review's *The Best 311 Colleges*, and propaganda by the pound from four different schools, we were hitting the road for the college tour.

We tested the seats to see how far we could recline. Way back. Cool. We got to laughing and had to squelch the noise out of respect for all the very quiet and dignified-looking people in business class. I imagined we were Peter Fonda and Dennis Hopper, reclining as if on chopped Harleys: Easy Rider blows through business class. Thumbs up, dude — this was going to be a romp.

Once we got rolling, Maggie went to make good on the free beverage business. "Get me a coffee," I said. A moment later she reappeared with two. I cocked my head quizzically. "You're drinking coffee?" She looked at me as if I must surely have been asleep for the last six months.

"Dad," she said with a sigh, "I've been drinking coffee for months."

Why was I so excited by this train trip? Didn't I know I was about to lose the last shred of parental influence with this child? Didn't I know that, by the time this girl and her kid sister flipped the graduation tassel, I would be forking over six figures? None of that even entered my mind as I watched the world slide by outside my window. This girl was on a journey and I was along for the ride.

We had hours to talk. About the kind of college she wanted to find, about her fantasy of campus life, about how she couldn't believe the clothes she was wearing a year ago, and how Mr. Castle, her history teacher, was completely blowing her mind. We talked about ideas and worldviews and immature boys.

When the train slid into the station, we grabbed our bags and headed into the city. As we approached the first college, she caught sight of the soaring Gothic halls and was smitten as surely as Hardy's young Jude Fawley pined for the distant spires of Cambridge. We walked the campus as the earnest student guide assured us that all classes were small, TAs were like hen's teeth, and real professors taught every class, came over to your table at Starbucks, and frequently entertained students for dinner. With prospects like these awaiting, I wondered if she could live another whole year with a little sister who was, well — a little sister, and parents who asked only if she had changed the kitty litter yet.

In the next two days we covered four colleges, traipsing

through classrooms (all equipped for PowerPoint presentations), student centers, dorm rooms (all Ethernet ready), cafeterias, and rec centers. Campus squares were full of kiosks plastered with posters for parties, lectures, avant-garde films, and political and religious tracts. It was one of those first-Christmas moments, when a parent lives to see a child's eyes bug out in wonder and delight. This time, however, I was privileged to introduce my daughter not merely to Disney World but to the real wonders of the world itself. I was happy just to be chauffeur and guide.

But something happened on the last day. Walking quietly through the study section of a great university library, I saw a young man lounging in an overstuffed chair, reading a novel, shoes off, legs thrown over the chair arms. Seeing this student, I felt an unmistakable twinge of envy. It had surely been building, deep in my subconscious, over the past two days — ever since we boarded the Silver Star. But it was only in that moment that I felt it and knew it. I wanted another crack at college. No, not exactly that. I didn't really want to go back. What I envied was the freedom to be in formation.

People just expect college kids to be on a journey, four years of adventure — intellectual, social, personal. But by the time we are old enough to drop our own children off at college, we are expected to be fully formed. We have already made our choices, gotten into one camp or another, become Republican or Democrat, pro-life or pro-choice, Baptist or Buddhist, VW or BMW. Standing before the young man in the armchair I wished I had not already made so many choices. I remembered what it was like simply to be free for the important questions. Was I too old for new ways?

I call that a Nicodemus moment, named for the wise, prestigious rabbi who, fascinated by Jesus, came to him by night. How can I be like you? he essentially said to the wonder-worker. And Jesus said, "You must be born again." In the presence of such wisdom, unfortunately, Nicodemus missed a few signs and got off at the wrong exit. Jesus was speaking of an inner transformation, yet this is the actual response of St. Nicodemus: "How can a man be born when he is old? Can he enter a second time into his mother's womb and be born?" I call him a saint because I take Nicodemus to be the patron of all those who would like to be transformed and born anew but wonder if maybe they aren't just a little too old for that kind of thing.

Back aboard the Silver Star, Maggie and I drank another free round of coffee. It was night. In a moment of silence she remembered her upbringing and thanked her father for taking the time and spending the money to make the trip possible. "Hey," I said dismissively, "this was as much fun for me as it was for you." Then we reclined our seats and rode for home.

Once More — Without Feeling

When my wife and I set out to learn how to dance, we did not expect to practice. We wanted to waltz like Maria and the captain in *The Sound of Music,* and we naively assumed that our expert instructor, Larry, would show us the basic trick to waltzing and then we would start twirling and gliding. Instead we spent half the hour learning how to rise and fall with every beat, how to place each step — *Drive with that foot,* he would insist, *No, heel first!*— and the other half learning three measly steps. (The poster board on the easel listed twenty-seven. We won't be waltzing in public until our silver anniversary.)

When the hour was up, Larry gave us a sheet with the twenty-seven moves and told us to go home and practice. "Next week," he said with a big smile, "I'll turn on the music and we'll start with a little dance recital."

The next day we put the coffee table in the hallway and moved the living room furniture against the walls. Practice began. Someone looking in the window (and don't think we didn't worry about that) would have seen two stiff mannequins locked in herky-jerky combat. But we were happily learning how to dance. For a week or more it was all wonderful like that.

It is not hard to dance with someone when everything

is just fine. But it is almost impossible to take up a dance position with someone you are fighting with. Pam and I tend not to have explosive fights. (I am Scandinavian and Virgo; I'm not sure what her excuse is.) Our quarrels tend to simmer for days until someone is grown-up enough to suggest we ought to have a talk.

In the middle of such a simmering conflict, however, it is time to go through our paces. "Are we going to practice our dance?" she says. "I guess so," I say with a passive-aggressive shrug. I put on the music and we stand in the middle of the living room floor like two hedgehogs negotiating an embrace. I take her right hand. Stiff. I place my right hand squarely on her back. She squirms as if in actual discomfort. Grand. We both want to say, "This is stupid — you can't dance with someone you don't even want to be in the same room with!" But we lurch forward on the downbeat of *Hi-Lilli, Hi-Lo,* clomping woodenly through the waltz. It is ugly, but we do it. And afterward we nod at each other coolly as if to say, "So there."

That dance rehearsal with its pathetic embrace was pure revelation. It may be impossible to dance with someone you don't even want to be around. But, we discovered, you can *practice* dancing. You don't always have to enjoy it, you just have to do it. It's the only way to become any good at this. When you're in conflict with your partner, you can't wait for reconciliation to hold one another and move in mirrored grace. You practice your way through the mess. In other words, dancers dance.

Because it involves intimacy, dancing seems to demand

emotion or feeling. Wrong. It's nice when feeling coincides with intimacy and the outward and visible beauty of a couple's movement seems a sacramental sign of an inward and spiritual grace. But don't hold your breath waiting for that one. It happens, but only because you practice.

We are sometimes enthralled by the romantic notion that, in intimate relationships, we ought not do or say anything we don't truly feel. To do so would be dishonest. Wrong again. Usually we have to go through the motions to get to the emotions. "We are more likely to act our way into feeling," C. S. Lewis said, "than to feel our way into acting." The twelve-steppers put it in shirtsleeve English: Fake it till you make it.

It is our family custom to hold hands when we say grace. We've done it since the children were old enough to join us at the table. Sometimes when we are in conflict, one or another person will decline to join hands. But more often than not we manage to close the circle. This act of intimacy does not mean that all parties are reconciled — the pitched argument continues right after the amen. It is simply a reminder that while we may be in a bitter war, we are fighting with those we dearly love. If action must wait upon feeling, it is impossible to hold someone's hand — and "insincere" to pray — in such a state of anger. Yet a moment's thought tells us that intimacy in the midst of conflict is the true test of love. Anyone can hold a hand or say a prayer when they feel like it.

In relationships, as in all of life, we are perfected by practice. It's the one thing we can do even if we're not sure we can do the real thing. If you can't dance, you can practice dancing. If you can't love, you can practice loving. If you can't empathize or set aside anger or hold a hand, you can practice doing it. Sometimes the other person can't tell the difference, and after a while, neither can you.

The Father's Toolbox

Not long ago my mother sent me a packet of old pictures. My parents have come to the point in life where they are giving things away while they can. Several months ago it was two pieces of Norwegian rosemaling that have always hung in my mother's kitchen. This time it was the pictures.

I knew them all. In our family if you say, "You know the picture of Jeanne smiling, with no front teeth . . ." we all know this is the picture from her sixth birthday party, when she received a brilliant orange tiger. And if you say, "Remember the one of John and David with Dad's toolbox . . ." we do not need to see the picture itself. We know. There are two young boys, two and four, with red cheeks and blue eyes, gleefully invading a big metal toolbox.

This was my father's toolbox. It was like a giant tackle box — half the size of a boy — that opened out into a series of smaller tiered trays. Here, in tidy array, were all the tools my father needed to repair televisions. An old black soldering iron, wire strippers, ohmmeter, little fuses that rattled in a hard plastic case, needle-nose pliers. I looked into the back end of a TV set and saw glass and plastic entrails. My father, like a surgeon, saw familiar anatomy. He restored dead things to life, and I thought he was a genius.

There I am with my little brother hovering over this chest of tools that work only in knowing hands. We want to have hands like that. In our little town my father was known as "TV Jerry." I wanted to grow up to be known and respected like him. I wanted to inherit his toolbox. But he did not make this easy.

I remember going on service calls with my father. Back when TVs were French colonial consoles designed to look like fine furniture, people didn't bring them in for minor repair. So my father made house calls. Sometimes he would take me along to some farmhouse out in Gayville, South Dakota. He introduced me as his helper. And when the farmer's wife asked me, "Are you going to be a TV man like your dad?" he always answered for me. I suppose I heard it a dozen times. "No," he would say, "he's going to do something important." That was his way of expressing his hope that I would give my life to God. To be a pastor, or even a missionary to Borneo. I knew then that I would never fix a single television.

I did not make it to Borneo. I am a pastor in Pennsylvania. I have tried to "give my life to God," but not, as it turns out, in the way my father and mother had hoped. Now when I see the boy standing over the father's toolbox, I realize how difficult it is to keep the fifth commandment: "Honor thy father and mother."

Every father wants the son to go beyond him. And — if you count things like advanced degrees — I have. I have even fulfilled in some way his hope that I would devote my life not to carrying his toolbox but to curing souls. But despite all that, there are times when I am afraid that I may never be what he is, or what he wanted me to be. He did not want me to follow in his footsteps, but he surely wanted me to stick to the family path. I suppose every generation delivers that mixed message to its children.

He did not want me tinkering with TVs, and he showed me the door that led beyond his shop next to the filling station in town. But he could hardly have guessed where I would go — and what all I would leave. I left his small town. I left his Swedish Baptist church. I spent four years in graduate school and learned just enough to recognize my former world as a distinct province. I went to divinity school and lost nearly every certitude he had given me. When I went home and he asked what I believed, I shaded my suspect new beliefs toward the old verities. I was afraid to disappoint him.

It is not easy to leave home, even when you've been shown the door. Like anyone else, I wanted my father's approval. Better, perhaps, to say that I wanted to keep my father's approval. I did not understand that a parent's approval must be tested to see what exactly is being smiled upon, the child in essence or the child compliant. I did not understand, of course, that with his right hand the father opens the door and gestures broadly toward the west, while with his left hand he is always holding the son by the belt loop. Even if the son has a very good father — and I do — the son who actually leaves will have to break away.

I begin to understand the ancient wisdom, "Therefore a man shall leave his father" . . . behind. Father-love half insists on it. And the son cannot shilly-shally at the door.

It has been over twenty years since I broke a belt loop. I live in a different world. I walk a road with few landmarks and fewer signs. Mostly I am happier. But I still have days when I wish I could live in my father's world. When I go wrong, when my children go wrong, I sometimes imagine that I am reaping the whirlwind — that I wouldn't be in this mess if I hadn't gotten on the slippery slope to begin with. It is then that I see my father, sitting at the kitchen table drinking coffee and "visiting" with me. I see how beautiful his white hair is. His fingers are a little crooked now and bulge at the joints, but they are still those knowing hands. His eyes are clear because he has lived with simplicity and integrity. This idealized image of my father comes to me when self-doubt arises. At moments like these I want to go home, and be the son again, and find that toolbox.

None of this would be a problem if my father were not, in his own world, a very good man. Decent, hardworking, devout, as good as his word — all the dogged farm virtues of the Midwest. I have always wanted to be as good a man as that. And when I question myself, when I regret the compromises I have made to live in the East, I want to go back to his world, where that kind of goodness still seems possible. I forget that the only man who can find goodness in that world is he.

If I want to honor my father I must get over my fear of doing what he called "something important." I must trust that Dad spoke the truth, without understanding the consequences, when he told the farmer's wife I was not going to do what he did. He showed me the door, withheld from me the old, black solder gun, the wire-strippers, the needle-nose pliers. He trusted me not to carry his toolbox. I suppose he figured I didn't need it. I was already carrying another set of his tools that would open to me a world of which he only dreamed.

A Grief Enacted

If my mother were to tell the story of her own death, she would have good material to work with. Mother was a good storyteller with a natural flair for the dramatic. "She had intense pain here in her abdomen," she would say. "And so they took her in for surgery. Told her husband and her seven children that it wasn't cancer, you know. Wasn't cancer. And then they opened her up and found her full of that cancer of the pancreas." She would shudder. "Nothing they could do. So they closed her up and sent her home — with hospice, you know. Four months later she died, poor thing."

I thought that when my mother died I would enter a state of grief. But when it happened I felt strangely powerless. How come I feel only emptiness? I used to think that grief was something that happened to you. Now I know it is something you must do.

What passes for grief is mostly a solemn, starchy affair. When my brothers and sisters and I accompanied my father to the funeral home to see my mother's body, we were ushered into a parlor with heavy drapery and small groupings of cocktail tables and wingback chairs. I felt as if I were visiting my mother at a strange and very wealthy neighbor's home.

Then I heard the low-level music. A lush version of "Our Day Will Come" was being played softly on a Hammond organ and a vibraphone. Aldoris Anderson knew nothing of contemporary culture and eschewed popular music. This was not sounding right. The music continued with "The Sound of Silence," "What Are You Doing for the Rest of Your Life" (both either oddly appropriate or in very poor taste), "Vincent" ("Starry, Starry Night"), "Feelings," "Theme from Mahogany" ("Do You Know Where You're Going To"), "Lara's Theme" (from *Doctor Zhivago*), followed by "Our Day Will Come" again. The tape was on a loop.

In some way, that epitomizes the grief process immediately after a death. The professionals take over and we are invited into their parlor. (I'm keeping that in mind the next time I welcome the bereaved into my office.) We are out of our element. We feel a little uncomfortable asking questions about the macabre, and it leads to a kind of quietism. We get dressed up and sit in those wingback chairs.

Not everyone, however, starts the grief process like this. There were twenty grandchildren, aged three to twenty-five, who made it home for my mother's funeral. They got all dressed up and did the viewing one day and the funeral the next. But at night they ate Grandma's signature Rice Krispie bars and played capture the flag, the same as they did every Fourth of July, every family reunion. They did not spend much time talking about Grandma or even about their feelings. We heard them shrieking and laughing and accusing each other of cheating. We went out to investigate reports of grave injury, and we listened to the littlest ones who came in seeking assistance for older siblings in "jail."

We saw how the cousins clung more closely together. It was as if they had discovered common blood and genes for the first time. "Look at our mouths," two cousins would say, "they're the same!" Mannerisms everywhere appeared identical. Even the annoying habit of picking food from a neighboring plate was traced relentlessly through bloodlines. They never spent so much time looking at the family pictures in the living room. And they kept to their traditions: eating Rice Krispie bars and playing capture the flag. This was how they enacted both their loss and their grandmother's continued presence in their own faces, in their own blood.

By the time six of my mother's grandsons carried her coffin to the grave, I was tired of doing nothing. I had sat through a service at the viewing and another at the funeral and a brief graveside prayer service after that. When the last prayer was said, and everyone had taken a flower from the casket spray and my father had given a red rose to every granddaughter, the funeral director nodded: it was time to go to our cars and go home. But we lined up for pictures and clutched our flowers, and said what a beautiful hill this was for a resting place. We weren't moving along.

I went to my father and asked if we could stay to watch the coffin lowered into the grave. If I wanted to, he said, it was fine. I went to the funeral director and he gave the high sign to the workers parked in a pickup down behind the trees. Things got quiet as two men placed a vault over the coffin and utterly silent when Mom began her descent into the earth. The funeral director flashed an earnest, terminal smile. Time to go? "Bring on the dirt," I said. And on came a tractor pulling a cart of earth. I took a handful of black dirt and let it fall between my fingers onto the white coffin. Thank God my hands were dirty. At least I could say I had helped bury my mother. Then we watched as the men filled the grave, packed the sides with their heels, and raked off the perfectly mounded tumulus. Then they left us alone.

I knelt down and brushed the dirt from the bronze marker with my hands. My fingers read the sharp, unweathered letters of her name and years. I pulled up the vase from the hole in the center, turned it upright and locked it into place. In a moment we were filling it with flowers, and tending the grave the way a husband and children and grandchildren ought to and need to. Then we wiped our hands clean with tissues and went home.

As a pastor I have always heard about the importance of "grief work," but I did not understand it until my mother died. It is not a passive process that happens to you. It is work. Or — in a beautiful and instinctual way for children — play. Either way, you have to get busy.

The Man Who Did Nothing

Not long ago I went home to visit my father for the first time since my mother died, earlier in the year. En route to the little airstrip in Sioux City, Iowa, the pilot's square-jawed voice interrupted the peanut service. Instead of coming in at gate two, he announced with a straight face, we were coming into gate one. I knew this little airport. It only had two gates and they were fifty feet apart. The woman in the next seat smiled in amusement, and I laughed out loud. But that slight gate change turned out to be a portent. My entry into the home my mother had vacated was, in its own way, not quite the same as it had always been.

My father met me with a hug and we surveyed one another. He was thinner and I was not. He tossed my bags in his car trunk and asked if I wanted to go out for some dinner. It was about ten-thirty. "I thought you would just take me home for goulash, molasses bread, and coffee," I said, rehearsing my mother's standard fare for late-night, homecoming travelers. We had a sad laugh, then he drove me to an all-night diner, patronized at that hour by truckers and other cowboys of the night.

Used to be my father would do the airport run; my mother never came out to meet us. She was always home, preparing for our arrival. And when we came in, everything was ready. I mean everything. The kitchen table was set, and the food was warming on the stove. It always seemed that she had rearranged the tchotchkes around the house to feature the things that I — and not the six other kids — had given her for Mother's Day and birthdays. She would meet me at the door as if I had been delivered by my father, who would come behind with my bags. My room was always prepared. Years ago she had turned the unfinished basement into a series of motel rooms, and mine would be made up. There were always notes on the dresser, telling me where to hang wet towels and not to wonder about the ticking sound in the night (the water meter was behind the bed). At family reunions we would compare room notes and howl.

When my father and I came home this night, nothing had been prepared. The place smelled different. Not bad, just empty. The dining room table, once vested in white and covered with plastic, was appointed with odd pieces of Tupperware and grilling tools. I thought my father was preparing for a yard sale, but he said it was just stuff he didn't know what to do with. Books and newspapers lay unbelievably on the living room floor. The refrigerator held orange juice, bagels, and Miracle Whip. When I asked for my room assignment, he told me to pick one. The linens were down there somewhere. I made up a bed at midnight in the room with the water meter. The note was still on the dresser. "Clicking sound is water meter in corner — John Charles was here 10/96 and thought it was a mouse. Ha!"

How exactly do we live now that the remarkable woman

who wrote such a note is gone? That was the unspoken question of our week together. Mother was everything, the unmoved mover. Not the one who picked you up, but the one who stood at the door. She was powerful in the old-fashioned way of women who had very low public profiles but who ruled the home. She was the impresario who mediated all family relationships: you were related to your father and your siblings through her. She wrote all the letters and did all the talking on the telephone. She told you what all the other kids were doing and her storytelling shaped and interpreted the events she recounted. How were we going to live in her pulsating absence?

All of the children were carrying more than a little anxiety about life after Mom. How would Dad take care of himself? He did not know how to cook, how to work the washer. That's what we whispered among ourselves. What we didn't talk about was the greater anxiety: How were we going to relate to Dad and to each other now that the telephone switchboard operator was gone. Forget the washer and the stove — Dad didn't know how to use the *phone*. And without that, what would hold us all together?

I must have assumed that my father would pick up my mother's role, or perhaps that was my hidden hope when I returned home. It should have occurred to me at the all-night diner, or when I saw the Tupperware all over the dining room table, but I didn't figure this out until I scrounged for sheets at midnight. Then the realization came. This guy had not turned a hand (as my mother would say) to prepare for me like I was the Prince of Wales. That was my mother's business, and it had not even occurred to him to try or to apologize for not trying. He had lost the morning and evening star of his life, and he best mourned that loss, I began to realize, by living with the clearest possible sense of her absence. Not by trying to fill that void. He said it best on the phone with someone who called to see how he was. "I'm not all right," I heard him say, "but that's okay."

Again and again the cohort of my eighty-one-year-old father's generation turns out to be wiser than the psycho-savvy generation of children who worry about them. I fairly chuckled to myself: This guy was just fine. In his quiet way he was simply going on. He knew what he couldn't do, what he couldn't be. In the face of our unuttered anxiety he merely trusted. Life without wife and mother was not all right, but that was okay. For this family, it would have to be. The phrase was foreign to his lips, but his life said, "Let it go. Let it be."

Epiphanies in

Ordinary

Time

☉

Plato's Garage

I don't know Larry that well. Our kids go to school together, and we're in a soccer car pool, which is how I ended up at his house to pick up my kids. "Come on in," he said, "the kids are upstairs — I'll tell them you're here." He was calling through the door from the garage into the house, so I walked in through the garage.

I took one step in and felt as if I'd fallen into the pages of one of those do-it-yourself books about the perfect workshop. I was overcome with awe.

I saw two bikes up on perfect racks, surgically straight, and I paused. Then I saw the garden hoses rolled and stowed with the kind of precision that brings tears to the eyes of a fireman, and I stopped. As if I were in a great cathedral, I looked up and turned slowly on my heels. All the garden tools, all the lawn chairs, all the everything was right where it was supposed to be. I've seen a few neat garages in my time, but Larry's beat all. (No wonder he so blithely beckoned me through the garage door.)

Apparently I stayed too long in adoration. A moment later Larry was at the door. "Thought you'd gotten lost," he said.

"No, I'm — fine," I stammered. I couldn't think quickly enough to explain why I was standing in his garage with my hands folded, so I broke down and told him the truth. "Wow," I said, gesturing widely, "your garage, Larry. It's so . . . beautiful."

If we humans could just enjoy a good garage whenever we run across one, and leave it at that, we might live in bliss. But inevitably that experience of flawlessness — that lofty vision of Plato's "D" realm — serves only to remind us that we mortals grind out our existence in a mere shadow of the perfect archetype. In short, we can't help making the comparison.

Which was pretty much what I was suffering on the way home from Larry's. I kept trying to remember if Larry had ever been in *my* garage. At the time, of course, it wouldn't have mattered enough to remember. But that was before I'd stumbled into his Platonic garage. Now I felt inadequate.

I had a friend in college who, when uppity people outdid him, would growl in his best Southern lockjaw, "Don't make me hate you!" It was a comedy routine for my friend, but we all knew the darker reality. We were laughing at our own insecurity. Whatever we were doing could be just fine — until we met someone who did it better. I felt my jaw locking and a growl coming on.

My rationalizing skills being what they are, I quickly reasoned that Larry's doctor-wife made him scrub and organize the garage every Saturday, and that was why it reminded me of a surgical suite. After that I reasoned that he had too much time on his hands and nothing better to do. After that I stopped reasoning and faced the fact that this had nothing really to do with Larry. It's just what happens when we try to size up our lives against some imagined standard.

Shakespeare captured the futility of such comparisons in one of his well-known sonnets.

> *Wishing me like to one more rich in hope,*
> *Featur'd like him, like him with friends possess'd.*
> *Desiring this man's art, and that man's scope,*
> *With what I most enjoy contented least* (Sonnet 29)

I *most enjoy* my garage as is (after all, my messy car demands no better). So why is this choice *contenting me least?*

Someone writing in shirtsleeve English said it equally well: "Never compare your insides to someone else's outsides." This is just the problem. We tend to externalize the inner qualities we desire, just because we can't stack up what we can't see. *I'm good if I look good. I'm strong if I appear that way. I'm rich if you think so. I'm wise if I sound it.* No matter that goodness and strength, richness and wisdom are cultivated in secret and manifest only to those, in Jesus' terms, with "eyes to see." To our eyes, you haven't got it if the world can't see it. So our efforts are poured not into inner, hidden cultivation, but into measurable affectation. Which puts us on that killer cycle. I show what I've got out there in the great bazaar of society, but as good as it is, I'm always seeing something "better." My goods are always being discounted by comparison.

When the kingdom comes we will no longer compare.

In the meantime we can hardly help it. The best we can do, it seems, is to know our vulnerability — to feel the jaw locking, the growl coming on — and to break the killer cycle. In my case, I ought to return to Larry's garage, genuflect and say, "It's perfect. It's just not me."

Trash Talk

Where I grew up there was an alley, bisecting the block, that ran behind our house. Among other things, that's where people put their trash cans.

We didn't "put out the trash." We put it behind a bunch of bushes in the alley where no one could see it. In fact, I can still remember my surprise at moving to a new town where, once a week, nice people in nice houses gathered all their wretched refuse and put it— of all places, I marveled — on their front sidewalk.

Sometimes I still feel a little funny putting out the trash. What we throw away tells a lot about us. (When I put out the recycling, I wave to my neighbors and tuck the wine bottles under the soda cans.)

If you take an early-morning walk, the way Pam and I do, you can hardly avoid trash shopping. Walking down the street— with oversized garbage barrels, recycling bins, and attic treasures lining the curbs — is like strolling the aisles of a bad boutique. Without really wanting to, I know which neighbors read *National Geographic* (all tied up in twine) and which ones had a party this week (let's hope it was only a party). I know who's remodeling their kitchen (a disposal and old, collapsed cabinets) and who just got a new NordicTrack.

On Tuesday evenings I put out the trash. It's one of the

rhythmic rituals of life that I actually enjoy. Having organized, dependable sanitation is one of those benefits of civilization that we just take for granted. On a good night, I don't. *Let us praise God for the trash man.* Is it just me, or does everybody enjoy getting rid of the week's offscouring? It feels good to get rid of junk. To get the paint cans out of the basement and the broken weed whacker out of the garage for good. Anything I can roll, haul, or drag to the curb by nightfall will be spirited away by morning. Is this not a borderline miracle?

Yet darker thoughts arise as well. Almost every time I carry our stuff to the curb, I am forced to consider the sheer weight and mass of all this family of four (and three cats) consumes. It's a stewardship moment. We bring home loads of stuff just because we can afford to, and a whole lot of it ends up in the trash. To lift the can is to heft my lifestyle.

I sometimes wish we still had alleys where we could all hide our life's jetsam. But maybe there's something to this weekly ritual of carrying out our junk and putting it on curbside display. You have to think about it. So you line it all up, take one final look, and walk away thanking heaven: In the morning, the trash man cometh.

Contemplative Gardening

I water the flower garden at night. It's better for the flow-ers, I know, but I water at night mostly because it's better for the waterer.

I am not a very good gardener, and I would probably get a C— in "The Principles and Practice of Contempla-tion." But somehow when the evening is quiet and cool, and I am sending a fan of water over the impatiens under the big spruce tree — somehow then I am a very good gar-dener and contemplation comes naturally.

This is so easy, delivering the water of life to these plants who would die without me. I am keeping the prom-ise implicit in my planting, and that feels good.

I hold the hose and envision roots finding water in the under darkness, and I just assume that after a scorching day flowers feel things like relief and gratitude. Flowers are great that way, you can project your feelings all over them and no one gets hurt.

Usually by the time I finish it is dark except for the porch light. Watering is entrancing, hypnotic: the spray goes back and forth, back and forth. I can't help thinking about my life and the lives of people I know. Analogies grow like weeds: flowers wilt, get distressed, need more or less sun, get transplanted and experience shock. Good flowers wind up in bad soil. Broken flowers come back,

sometimes. It's all just like people. The same mystery ob-
tains. All things being equal, some flowers flourish and
some don't, and no one can say why.

Nevertheless, amid the thicket of analogies I water on
in the glow of the porch light. It is easy as the waterer to
think about all that is flourishing and dying in my life. Because this is a time to *do* absolutely nothing, I can think
about the nagging problems. Nothing needs to be done
right now; nothing can be.

Sometimes, at some point, I discover I have crossed the
dim line between watering-and-thinking and contempla-
tive prayer. The waterer becomes the watered-upon. The
life-giver receives. And that is when we know that prayer
is a gift of God. So often when we try, nothing happens. So
we are invited just to clear a space and stop trying. Clear a
space — plant a seed — keep watering.

The End of the Clothesline

The clothesline that stretched from my grandmother's farmyard to every backyard in Yankton, South Dakota, where I was raised, reached the end of the line when I got to college. There I learned to throw clumps of wrung-out clothes into the gaping maws of the dryer, close the hatch and buy fifty cents' worth of sunshine.

I had not thought much about the end of the clothesline until we had to do laundry on vacation in Nova Scotia. The place had a washer all right. But the dryer was definitely a series of ropes strung out in the backyard.

I found the clothespins and was headed out into the sunshine when my teenage daughter caught me at the door. "Don't tell me," she said with a truly confused look in her eyes, "that you are going to hang my underwear out there for the world to see." (Five other condominiums shared the same backyard.) I laughed. "There's no dryer. Where *else* do you suggest we hang it?" and I leaned into the door. She caught my arm. This was serious. "Wait," she said, eyes now hooded with malice. "Don't you dare hang my things out there."

After a brief negotiating session, with both necessity and reality on my side, we reached an agreement: her things in back.

By the time I finally laid my basket in the grass beneath the clothesline, the unexpected struggle at the door had heightened my awareness. Hanging clothes on the line — something my mother had taught me as a boy in a family of nine — was still second nature. Like riding a bike. I curled the very tippy tip of the sock over the line and clamped it; I secured the shirt, upside down, with a pin at each seam on the shirttail, then stretched out the wrinkles. The way Mom taught me. I had not taught this to my daughter. Maybe she'd thrown a beach towel over a line in Florida, but she'd never hung out a single sock. We didn't have a clothesline. None of her friends did. No wonder she was aghast to see me headed into the public domain with the Anderson laundry.

Everybody in my hometown had a clothesline. We knew about dryers, of course, but my mother did not believe in them. She said they ruined your clothes. Maybe it was sour grapes because we could not afford a dryer, but necessity forced us — and everybody else in our neighborhood — to hang our clothes out in public. And since everybody did it, nobody had quite my daughter's drop-jawed response.

Virtue is born of necessity. We did not take up clothespins in order to open ourselves to the world, even our rather private selves — our dirty laundry, boraxed and blued as best we could. But that was the effect. Whole family wardrobes waving in the breeze were a common symbol of an unconscious and universal community.

My daughter's near mortification reminded me of how private we've become. I thought of the woman who told me that her husband refused to go to an AA meeting because he could handle this *on his own.* Besides, he'd been to one of those ghastly groups, and all they did was tell their sad little pathetic stories. I guess he didn't want to hang out his laundry with everyone else's.

I recalled the woman I met one summer who told me she stopped going to church because people were too eager to shake her hand and introduce themselves. "I don't go to church to meet *people*," she said. "I go to church to meet God." I didn't know we had to choose between the two. But she wanted to go it alone.

I thought of how, when illness or calamity strikes, we lock ourselves in a room, afraid to tell anyone for shame or fear. What if our friends offer to *help*?

While I may yet string up a clothesline in our backyard, I'm not likely to give up our Maytag. But I hope I'll never again throw a load in the dryer without remembering what this time-saver is costing me. That's one less trip into the world where the sun and wind must be my friend, and where my neighbor, mowing his yard, might just notice that all my whites are a little gray and a few of my socks have holes, too. Just like his.

Playing for Life

There is a playground in town. I pass it often during the week. And lately when I do I've been slowing down to watch the kids skimming down the silver slide, urging the merry-go-round to warp speed, teetering lazily on the see-saw, and swinging. The swings are best of all. On a swing a kid has wings.

Not long ago on a summer afternoon when the playground was full and whirling like a carnival, I pulled over and stopped. Mothers and fathers were sitting at picnic tables, coaxing timid children down treacherous slides, pushing the littlest ones in the safety-seat swings. I saw it all through my window like a silent drive-in movie.

Of course I asked myself what in the world I was doing, stopping along the road like this. I figured it was a lot of things. My girls don't ask me to take them to the playground anymore. And I was fascinated by mere play — something I don't do much anymore, even though mental health experts have for some time been telling this work-obsessed culture that adults need play time, too. I know how to take time off, but that's not the same as playtime.

So it came as no great revelation that I was stopped along the road, watching this pell-mell world of play, because I wanted to be on that swing set. I smiled to myself, shook my head, and didn't think much about the swings again until lunch after a funeral one Saturday.

We had just sung and prayed our farewells to Bill, a pastor for over fifty years, a college professor and dean, author, musician — a true polymath. And now we were sitting under tents in the summer sun, having lunch, meeting folks who knew Bill in different eras of his life and in different contexts. And telling stories of course.

I told how Bill mentored me as a young pastor, and someone else remembered Bill the philosopher and theologian. But the story that swung me smack-dab back into the playground came from a woman who used to be an organist at a parish where Bill was serving. She came to church early one Sunday morning, she said, and found Bill in the playground — lazing on the swing set. He wasn't the least embarrassed, she said, a man in his sixties then. He didn't feel any need to explain. He simply wished her a good morning and kept on swinging.

That was a moment when I sensed a message had been delivered. I listened because I have this fear that if I regard these moments with predictable skepticism, God will figure after a while that it's no use trying to get through to me. I knew where I had to go.

When I got there the place was half empty as I slipped in the gate and made for the wide-open swings. One little girl on the safety swings looked over her shoulder, pointed at me, and said something to her mother. Only the boughs of a great maple saved me in my gray funeral suit from the white sun. I pushed off with my heels, then retracted my legs like landing gear, opening them anew as beating wings. I rose.

Only trouble was, I got dizzy and my stomach did a wheelie. Too much funeral food. And too little time on the swings these days. At the peak of my yearning I wondered how I ever used to "bail out" at high altitude.

After a brief flight my heels touched down and I came to rest. I sat on the swings in memory of Bill while the stark admonition of the Burial Office spun in my head: "Make us, we pray, deeply aware of the shortness and uncertainty of human life . . . ."

Never too short for work, of course, and never too uncertain for duty. But if I learned to work like an adult I suppose I must learn to play like one. As I sat in the swing, I tried to remember when it felt good to be dizzy, when I swung until the sun went down and the yellow streetlights flickered my curfew. Then, without thinking, I pushed off with my heels again and felt dizzy and alive.

Keeping Time

The idea was partly my own, and it seemed simple at the time. We needed to understand and assess the work of our staff — including many volunteers who, almost invisibly, put in hundreds of hours. So we decided to ask every staff person and regular office volunteer to do a time study. Just keep track of everything you do, and how long it takes you to do it. For a month. As I say, it sounded simple enough.

We were all handed an elaborately simple form. Date. Activity. Time spent. Location (office, church, home, other). Comments. And Code — someone would enter all this into a computer. Each activity, then, needed to be coded so the data could be analyzed.

There were a few jokes around the water cooler that day, but we all got to work on our time studies. I sat at my desk, dated my first sheet, and forgot all about it until five-thirty. Maybe tomorrow, I thought. But tomorrow brought a funeral and two deadlines. At the end of the day I tried to reconstruct my time. It was hopeless and I vowed to begin on Monday morning.

The basic problem with keeping track of my time, I discovered when I finally got down to business, is that it demands a kind of hyper-consciousness. While I'm opening my mail I'm thinking, *Now I am opening my mail. I had better jot this down on the sheet.* This of course is not

normal. Most of life is spent on mindless tasks. I fix my
balky stapler without knowing it took me ten whole minutes. I daydream. I file old finance committee notes. I read
junk e-mail while I'm on hold listening to Barry Manilow
singing "Mandy" on my speakerphone. I come home after
a day like that and someone asks what I did today. I mutter,
"Just cleaned up my desk," as I doff my collar and start
riffling through the day's mail.

It's not normal to be conscious of all the little things,
but it is in fact critical. The obvious but overlooked fact of
life is, it's *all* little stuff. There is a big picture, yes, but it's
a pointillist masterpiece. Viewed at close range, the figures, colors, and shading are just a billion dots.

You clean up the breakfast dishes, call your mother, fill
the bird feeder, make more coffee, and what happened to
the day? We live mindlessly. That's not an indictment, just
a fact. Without some spiritual practice (or office time
sheet) to keep us focused on the present moment, we in-
variably slide either backward or forward. We worry about
the past; we seek to relive what has been. Or we live for the
future. In this mind-set, what we do all day is not the
point. The real point is what we're working toward. Like
the blue-collar heroes of countless beer commercials, we
are working all day to get to "Miller Time." Which may in
fact be five o'clock and a drink to escape the mindlessness,
or it may be the weekend trip, the graduation or the wedding, the promotion or the move. We are taught to see life
falsely as a succession of big events or episodes, and we
miss the life we are actually living in the meantime.

"Wake up," Jesus said, "and stay awake." In Buddhist

language it is "mindfulness." Rather than skipping over the mundane to get to the supposedly big events, we are encouraged to be mindful of whatever we are doing in the moment. Washing up the breakfast dishes isn't just a mindless must-do, it's a sacred moment if we do it fully awake and aware. In all religious traditions, the door to the numinous stands in the ordinary.

I am three weeks into my time-accounting regimen. With a week to go I have finally stopped fighting it. It was never presented as a spiritual practice, but that is what it has become. Anything that keeps us continually aware of life in the present moment is a spiritual practice. In fact, keeping time for twenty-one days has been more effective than my standard prayer time, where I seek to open myself to the immediate presence of God, dismissing all distracting thoughts that pull me from the moment. The time sheet in the corner of my desk has me more aware than ever that I am right now standing at the copier, duplicating a letter, and this is a good thing to be doing. I am standing in the hallway talking to someone about arthritis, and this is my calling for now. I am on the phone with the school nurse discussing a daughter's stomach pains, and this is my momentary job description. I am frequently frustrated by the little distractions that seem to keep me from bigger things. But if God is in the details, what's wrong with these?

Against the popular concept of "time management," which encourages multitasking and high-speed efficiency, keeping time reminds me that every task is holy and — what's more — things take as long as they take. I can "get more done" only by refusing to be mindful of the one thing I am doing right now.

Which, in my case, is writing a piece on Saturday afternoon to satisfy a last-Tuesday deadline. I can kick myself for several attempts that failed for lack of inspiration, and imagine that I am doing on the weekend what I *should* have been able to do during the week. But the simple fact is, it took me as long as it took me, and I am about to jot that on my time sheet with a shrug and a sigh.

Forget the Code

The other day I happened to be in the doctor's office, waiting of course. It was quick from the waiting room to the examination room, but the real wait was for the doctor. The friendly nurse ushered me into a little room, pulled fresh paper over the exam table, and invited me to sit on it. I felt like a puppy. She closed the door behind her as she left, assuring me the doctor would be with me in just a jiffy. I nodded and played along. Why did I leave my magazine? I thought. I sat on my paper until boredom set in. That's when I saw the form hanging on the wall over the sink. I got up to go read it.

At the top it said, "Diagnostic Code." There in no particular order were all the disorders we suffer — with a code attached. There was "Croup." It's code? 464.4. "Wart" was 078.1. "Gallbladder," 575.9. There was even a code for "Anxiety," 300.00.

I felt as if I were reading something the patient is not supposed to see. So *this*, I thought, is how they talk about me after I pay my bill and leave. "He's not sick, just a case of 780.7" ("Malaise Fatigue").

This intrigued me. Did it merely depersonalize? No. More than that. It pathetically oversimplified.

I heard a noise in the hall and quickly sat down on the exam table. It wasn't the doctor (of course). Wouldn't it be nice, I thought, if "Malaise Fatigue" were really as simple as 780.7? But those codes are only good for insurance forms. They are of no use to any of us.

How far would I get assigning codes to people who sat in my office? You can't find a job and can't get out of bed? That's definitely a 367.7. Your grown daughter returns your letters unopened? Got to be a 523.4. Can't pray anymore and feel empty inside? 296.5.

The first step to wisdom, the Chinese say, is getting things by their right name. The next step is knowing what cannot be named, and certainly not coded.

We all have friends or relatives who want to "code" our problems. They know just what ails us and what we ought to do or take or abstain from taking. Ask anyone who's been seriously ill. Everybody's got the elixir. Everybody's best friend had the same thing you have and got rid of it with something off the Internet. When my mother lost her second child at a mere twenty-six days, plenty of Job's comforters came by to assure her she was actually better than she knew. At least the child did not suffer. She would have another baby. And so on. Only one friend, she told me, understood that nothing could be said, nothing could be done. It was a grief beyond expression.

She relearned that lesson later in life. When a friend of the family lay gravely ill, my mother told me, she stood outside the hospital room because she did not know what to say. Another friend came to visit and my mother watched as she entered the room, knelt down by the bed, and said simply, "Marilyn, I love you." "Now, why didn't I think of that?" she said to me.

What we all need is not someone who can name our affliction, much less fix us, cure us, tell us to look on the bright side. We all want someone who will only *be* with us. Someone — if we're very lucky — with a large enough soul to sit with intractable problems and not say a word. Every happiness, to paraphrase Tolstoy, is alike, and every suffering unique. This is not a problem to be solved; this is the mystery that defines normal human experience. And in the face of such a mystery, what is called for is reverent silence.

Don't be surprised, though, if it's terribly hard work, and you're soon back to diagnosing and prescribing. It's a nervous reaction: if you don't know what to say, say *some*-thing. It takes practice to nod quietly instead, sigh, and leave it at that. So let the doctors and insurance providers keep their hard numbers. We will observe a code of silence.

Plea Bargaining Heaven

Lawrence Township Municipal Court, Lawrenceville, New Jersey.

I am here at 9:45 A.M. for my appointed court date to fight a traffic ticket. I am scheduled for ten but am early. A woman at a desk outside the courtroom waves me in. I take my seat in a pew. A long wooden panel that stretches across the front of the room functions like a sanctuary rail, behind which, on a raised dais, sits a man in a black robe with an ornate crest on the wall above his head. I feel oddly at home: this feels a lot like church.

The service is already in progress and I sit quietly in the back. A young man approaches the bench — what looks to me like the altar. The judge says, "Good morning," but the boy only nods. He stands with legs splayed, hands behind his back. (In his hands he clutches a silver cell phone.) In a tired, Mirandizing tone the judge reads the charge: stealing a pair of khaki pants valued at $29.99 from J. C. Penney. How does he plead? Guilty, the boy says. The judge sips from his coffee mug. Does the young man understand that he can demand a trial; that he can get an attorney; that if he cannot afford one, the court must appoint one for him? The boy nods, persisting in his guilt. I wonder why he doesn't say a word in his defense.

Ten o'clock comes and goes. I watch as one man faces

charges of shoplifting and possession of marijuana. The next woman is charged with illegal trespass. Another man is accused of driving off without paying for car repairs in the amount of $4,026.79. They all plead guilty with no discussion.

At last the prosecutor calls my name and motions for me to meet him off to the side. He is a young man with a fresh suit and haircut to match. Behind us at the bench the wheels of justice grind on, and we speak in hushed tones. I am charged with reckless driving because I was driving down the middle of the street. True, I admit, I was driving down the middle of the street. But only, I explain in a vigorous whisper, because cars were parked on both sides of this narrow street and people had put their trash out on the street to boot. I am innocent of this charge, I say. He smiles in patronizing amusement. No attorney? No, I say. No knowledge of New Jersey law, the peculiarities of this court, and of this judge in particular? No, I say. Please, he says, and offers me a deal. Only eighty bucks and no points on my license.

I had thought I would stand before TV's Judge Judy or Judge Wapner of *The People's Court* and explain why I was right and the officer was wrong. The judge and I would have a talk. Can't I just explain what happened? I ask, pointing to the judge. I could do that of course, but that's considered a trial, the prosecutor patiently lectures me. Am I prepared to wait most all day for my trial — especially since I have no attorney and no knowledge of the law? Am I prepared to pay close to three hundred dollars if I lose (counting an insurance hit)? Why not pay the eighty and leave and enjoy the rest of the day? This is a shakedown, I complain.

The deal I am offered requires that I sit down and wait my turn, then stand in front of the judge and plead guilty to the lesser charge of "delaying traffic." I ask what that means; the prosecutor's shrug tells me it doesn't matter. I hesitate and my eyes plead, But what if I'm truly innocent? His head drops and his eyes remonstrate, C'mon, can't you see I'm busy here?

I go back to my pew with a better understanding of how this thing works. The boy with the silver cell phone said nothing before the judge because he had already worked out a deal with the prosecutor. We all had. This is how the system works, at least for petty criminals like us. First you see the prosecutor. He's the one who can reason with you, explain the system, and give you your odds. He's got power to make a deal. You can refuse it, of course. But once you spurn his offer and go before the judge, you take your chances. It will almost certainly be tougher on you. So everybody who can cops a plea.

When my time comes I stand before the judge and utter our prearranged lie. I understand that there's not enough time or money for every little offense to get a real hearing, and that the system has to discourage trials. Still, it feels wrong. I just want a chance to tell my story.

What else is bothering me here? It is sitting in a pew looking up at the judge in his solemn black robe. Church and religion can feel a lot like this. Churches have rules and laws, even ecclesiastical courts. And in the church people are pretty much presumed guilty.

I do not mean that no one was actually guilty in that courtroom. And I do not mean that, where God and the church are concerned, people are not ever morally guilty. We are. What feels wrong is how much the church's response to people's mixed up lives is just like the state's. The church has its own system, where the church brokers between poor sinners and their God. The rules are the rules, and one size fits all. A woman told me once that she stopped going to her church twenty years ago when her husband divorced her. She knew the rules; by the church's standards she was now an outcast. Her "innocence" would mean nothing.

When people run into trouble in life, they just want to tell their story. It may not be perfect — they're just playing the hand they've been dealt. But in the church we don't have time to listen to one soul's particular story or weigh extenuating circumstances. My God, we'd be here all day. And once we start making exceptions here and exceptions there, the whole thing starts to fall apart.

Exactly.

The Sabbath Habit

After Lent, Holy Week, and Easter, I always feel like I could use a couple of months' rest. This year I got it. After the last Easter liturgy I got in my car and headed for the Carolina coast. That week on the water with my family was the opening of a four-month sabbatical. Halfway into the longest period I ever spent away from the world of work — and let's face it, in America work is pretty much the world — I remember the Sabbath.

Sabbatical, after all, derives from *Sabbath*. God — yes even God — had to rest after a six-day workweek spent creating, well, the universe. Dog tired, God sat down and did nothing but admire. And since it did wonders for the Creator, God made it mandatory for us. "Six days you shall labor and do all your work," the word came down, "but the seventh day is a Sabbath to the Lord your God; in it you shall not do any work." In other words, "Remember the Sabbath day, to keep it holy."

After eight and a half years in service, I was in need of rest. Actually, I didn't know how tired I was until I sat down. Then I understood my need for a kind of rest that goes beyond taking a couple days off. I seemed to hear my mother. Whenever someone felt a malaise that couldn't be diagnosed as any particular malady, she would always say,

"Your body knows what it needs." I rolled my eyes when I was younger, but not anymore.

Most of us are not adept at listening to our bodies — or our minds or our spirits, for that matter (which is why we struggle so with prayer). We live in a world where such attentiveness is not merely undervalued, it is nearly forbidden. The market values workers who will gut out crazy hours and call it commitment, take a pill instead of a rest. If you've got a problem with that and pause for a moment to think about it, there's always someone waiting to cut in and run off with your job.

Get it straight: nothing in our culture supports the notion of Sabbath. If you want to live in a cycle of work and ritualized rest, you are on your own. Most of us remember when stores closed every day at five-thirty and all day Sunday. Today "blue laws" — which once limited commerce and established rhythms of work and rest — seem vaguely Victorian. Now the stores are always open; we're always working. If you want to check your bank balance, trade stocks and go shopping at two in the morning — log on! The market runs 24/7/365. It knows nothing of Sabbath.

And if we are slaves to work, we are willing victims. Some few of us are working overtime or holding down two jobs just to pay the rent. But most of us are working longer and harder not only because our avarice (now so common as to appear normal) demands it, but also because we are addicted to work. We go home when we have to, to keep spouses and children mollified. But as soon as we can slip away, we're back on the phone or online. Sociologist Arlie

Russell Hochschild writes, "The emotional magnets beneath home and work are in the process of being reversed." If we were honest, all those bumper stickers might say, "I'd Rather Be Working." (And thanks to cell phones, of course, time in the car need not be time away from work.)

We either flatter or deceive ourselves if we believe we are the first generation to struggle so painfully with the balance of work and rest. There's a reason why keeping the Sabbath is one of the ancient Ten Commandments. It's a divine *order* because rest has never been something we do naturally. Fear of privation, whether of food for the table or a vacation home at the shore, has always driven people to work seven days and skip the vacation. So God has always had to insist on rest. Flip the CLOSED sign, park the rig, shut down the computer. Take a break.

The joy of my long sabbatical had me anticipating the day it would end. I didn't want to return to work in the same old way. I wanted to continue the Sabbath habit, so that I could develop daily and weekly patterns of work and rest. We all fear that taking a break will make us less productive. The truth, of course, is both opposite and obvious.

The grace of my extended respite also made me a Sabbath advocate. As I talked to people about my own sabbatical, I encouraged others to take a sabbatical in whatever form they could. Ministers and college professors are not the only people who need sabbaticals. Mothers who "only work at home" need sabbaticals. Children and young people, we hear over and over, are stressed to the max and in need of a good long rest. Since retirement no longer means R&R, even retirees need sabbatical.

But listen to me, preaching as if this is some new discovery: everyone needs a sabbatical. It's as simple as the Fourth Commandment: Keep the Sabbath. That means everybody. Right up there with Do not steal, Do not commit adultery, Do not kill, God says: Do not work all the time. And that's an order.

Breathing Lessons

I never pictured myself on a cruise ship vacation. The reasons — beyond *The Love Boat* — are not important. The point is, I went on one the week after Christmas and loved it.

I ate well, nine times a day. I saw my children only at the evening meal. I sat alternately in the sun and in the whirlpool. I read three books I got for Christmas. I sat with my wife on the top deck in the moonlight as the sea rolled by and the band played "The Blue Danube Waltz" two decks beneath us. Yes, in the course of a week I had to listen to reggae music and dodge a few conga lines, but this is still good.

The best moment, however, was the unexpected one. We docked at Cozumel, Mexico, and caught a cab to Chankanaab National Park, there to loll on the beach. We set up camp under a shade palm, and I went to inquire about snorkel gear. The water was the green-blue color of some shocking tropical drink, and unseemly creatures were reputed to be everywhere in it. "How much for snorkeling?" I said. But this man had seen a billion tourists like me and had obviously learned not so much to listen to the request as to watch the eyes. I was asking about snorkeling but looking straight at the scuba gear.

You call this one. For eight dollars I get flippers and a

mask with a foot of garden hose that allow me to lie on my stomach all day and sunburn my pale back. For forty dollars I get to be a porpoise for an hour.

I have always fantasized about solo flight and scuba diving. Humans have been denied the heights of the sky and the depths of the sea, and I have always wanted to enter those two realms with as little between me and the elements as possible. It didn't count that I had been on plenty of planes and even a nuclear submarine. I wanted the immediate experience.

Fernand was the Mexican man who was offering to cut the price, teach me how to scuba in thirty minutes, and be the dive instructor and guide for my hour undersea. I hurried back to the suntan camp, and in less than a minute I was back with Pam. Fernand smiled and got us our gear. "What size shoe?" he asked, sizing me up for flippers. I told him twelve. "Oh, señor," he said, "you don' *need* flippers!" I was going to love this Mexican Cousteau.

I never listened so closely for thirty minutes in my life. I learned how to equalize the pressure in my ears, how to clear my mask of water, how to adjust the buoyancy in my vest, how to remove and retrieve my regulator underwater, how to check my oxygen level. I learned five hand signals: OK. Something's wrong . . . with my ears, my mask, my regulator. Up/down. Low on oxygen. And finally, how to report to Fernand the approximate oxygen level in my tank. Then we strapped on twelve pounds of belted lead weights and got into what felt like a fifty-pound vest, tank attached.

Lumbering toward the water I felt like a herky-jerky

figure in an old newsreel, one of those crazy men in fabulous contraptions jumping off small cliffs in hopes of flight. I was about to attempt, if not the impossible, then at least the improbable. I thought I might panic, especially when I had to take off my lifeline underwater, toss it behind me while slowly exhaling ("We never hold our breath under water . . ."), get it back in my mouth, clear it of water, and start breathing again. I suppose I knew I would be in only twenty feet of water, and the worst that could happen would be sore ears if I panicked and made for the surface.

But it did not feel that way when I put on my supplemental flippers, and splashed like a rock into the salt water. Lead belt, vest, and tank pulled me under, and I thrashed instinctively to keep my head above water. I went under again and held my breath. I bit down on the regulator, not trusting that I could take a breath. Can you blame me? In forty plus years I had not taken a breath underwater. Then *Hs-s-s-s.* I heard the air pour into my lungs.

For the next hour we slid along the ocean floor, over coral reefs and underwater sand dunes. It was like swimming in a pet shop aquarium, with wild and weird fish wandering by. A black and yellow striped thing passed me with a bug-eyed glance. I reached out tentatively, vainly. I followed Fernand into the mouth of a cave, and through a shimmering silver wall of sardines, a wall that bent with our approach and finally burst into a cave where two twelve-foot tarpons were feeding — on sardines. I did not know what they were and what they ate. I immediately assumed they were sharks who were happy to eat me, and for the second time I held my breath. But Fernand was calm and I breathed again. *Hs-s-s-s.*

I was never more than thirty feet down, but the line between my world and this world, the fish world, was passed when I took my first breath below sea level. For an hour I was mindful of — and thankful for — each breath. I could hear it coming in with a clean *Hs-s-s-s,* and going out with a turbulent *Poosh-sh-sh,* as a rumble of bubbles poured out of my lifeline and fluttered for the surface. I did not think about anything on land. Only what was brilliantly before my eyes and what I could hear with my ears. *Hs-s-s-s* and *Poosh-sh-sh.* Yes, I am breathing. *Hs-s-s-s* and *Poosh-sh-sh.*

I have taken breaths by the billions, without so much as a thought. And yet in that one undersea hour I treasured every delicious lungful. Why can I not live and breathe like that on land? I race through my life as if fleeing a mad pursuer. Eye on some distant prize, I miss the particulars that surround me on every side: the slivered moon and the frozen silence of the morning's walk. The smell of fresh newsprint when the paper hits the breakfast table. The scrim of steam on the bathroom mirror when I shave.

All this is lost on us who are always on the way to some greater achievement. Sometimes in the fevered rush we can hardly stop to take a deep breath. I know a man who put an unusual screen saver on his office computer. One word floats across the window: *Breathe.*

Respiration, it turns out, is the key to concentration. We lose touch with the present moment, when we lose track of our breathing — the actual in-spiration of God.

All the great spiritual guides begin the practice of prayer with the simplest exercise of all. *Breathe in and breathe out. This is the time-tested way to enter the present, where God is. It is how our bodies relax. Breathe in and breathe out. Listen to the air coming in and the air going out. And do not think of anything else. Do not regret the past or fear the future. Empty your mind so that you can be fully present to this moment.*

I can assure you that I did not go scuba diving in order to learn how to pray. I did not plunge into the marine world in order to learn how to pay attention. But when I was forced to breathe underwater, I had no choice.

Press Pause

"I wasn't feeling too well," she told me. "Feeling a little run-down; I'd get depressed. But I figured I was just out of shape. I ought to get out there and work a little harder."

Looking back, she thought, this had been going on for two years, but she just kept at it.

"Of course, I had so much to do."

Then the doctor spoke. Menopause.

"You know," she told me, "I think that means we're supposed to pause."

Meno-pause. The word, broken in two, struck me with new force. How plainly wise. By simply listening to the word itself, my friend had discovered that menopause was not merely something to be gotten over. It was sign and portent, hot-flashing harbinger of some new thing. If our bodies were like cars, red lights would flare on the dashboard: "Something important is happening to you. Please slow down and attend to it. You don't get to the next phase until you attend to this one."

The body tells us these things. So why was my friend ashamed to take a nap? Why do I fight my rising blood pressure, as if it were an alien force and not my own body? Something has taught us to ignore or override our inner voice. Why can't we pause?

Any old VCR knows the difference between stop and

pause. Sometimes we don't want to stop (sometimes we can't), but we need to pause. Take some time to know this empty feeling: can this really be filled by anything at the mall? Time to find out what this ache is all about: is this just backache — or heartache felt along the back? Half the drugs advertised on TV are substitutes for "pause." Take this and you won't have to think about why you're in pain. Hit the symptoms and head for work.

Men, especially, want to "play through pain," like the big guys in football pads. Naturally, they grow up numb. Women have their own ways of absorbing pain, storing it deep in forgotten cisterns. Distorting nature, we have made natural defense mechanisms and survival instincts into cultivated personal virtues: Successful people just keep on running, no matter what. They don't stop.

Which ought to give us pause.

A Good Cry

The plane was full, which meant there were 266 of us hustling to stake out a seat. People were clogging the aisles trying to jam oversized bags into overhead bins. Flight attendants were doing their professional best to referee the general shoving match in English, Spanish, and Italian. When everyone was belted in place, and the captain apologized for the delay, a baby began to cry somewhere behind me. Maybe ten rows back.

And would not stop. After five minutes the cry turned to a scream. People began looking at one another peevishly. One flight attendant came down the aisle with a bottle of water; another came with cookies and makeshift toys. The scream turned to a heaving, rolling wail of desperation.

I could see a bevy of flight attendants gathered helplessly, until a young steward came down the aisle. I heard him speaking fluent Spanish, and in a moment he had assessed the crisis: in the crowded plane, the baby's parents had been split up — the father's assigned seat was in the back of the plane. The steward quickly worked a trade (the man sitting next to mother and child happily gave up his seat) and reunited the family. Immediately — as if the power to an amplifier had suddenly been pulled — the baby's shrieking ceased. There was a moment of silence and then 264 passengers broke into spontaneous applause.

We clapped for the end of the noise and for the heroic diplomacy of the steward. But we also clapped because it was moving to see a hysterical child calmed in an instant by the presence of the father.

The sudden silence, however, was like a photographic negative, suggesting its opposite. The desolate howls resounded in my head. It was raw. Honest. Persistent. Effective. Here was a child crying inconsolably for security, raging against loss, against vulnerability — the close jarring and jawing of a hundred strangers.

I can still hear that baby's cry. I know I have heard it before, and not only from an infant. I have heard it in the ER, standing with a man whose wife had collapsed and been rushed to the hospital. As he received the news that his beloved was dead, he cried out in shock. I held him as he reeled and doubled over, heard the heaving cries that come up from the belly.

And I have heard that cry when there was nothing left in the belly, no breath left to climb the throat. The woman who sat in my office with her husband, the man who was up and leaving. He spoke calmly, rationally. She had wept herself to utter exhaustion and literally could not speak. Finally her terror came out in a whisper, a death rattle more disturbing to me than the loudest ululation of the baby in the airplane.

I keep hearing echoes of that child's cry because it was so clear. Babies, naturally, are very good at crying, and this tiny human with the oversized woofer seemed to give

voice to all the fears and anxieties that bedevil us. Our
world is too much like that jet packed with strange people
elbowing for space in the languages of Babel. Change, loss,
separation, dark monsters, real and imagined. It would
help if we could face these old fears and feel the catharsis
of a good rant, whether we were in the presence of anyone
else or alone.

But at our age we are not good criers anymore. Some
complain that we have become a society of crybabies.
Maybe whiners and sulkers and gripers, but not real wail-
ers. We are not gifted enough to let fly with "My God, my
God, why have you forsaken me? and are so far from my
cry and from the words of my distress?" (Psalm 22). Or to
shock everyone from first class to the rear galley with the
poetic howl of Dylan Thomas, who urged we not go gentle
into the good night but instead "rage, rage against the dying of the light." No, it takes a mighty, mighty crier to
retch up anything so true and cold.

The essential irony of spirituality is that we mature by
becoming more childlike. This means, I think, that we can
learn something from that crying baby. If we hear it and
feel oddly envious of the raw honesty and energy of it all,
we can start by acknowledging that. There are many
adults who wish they could cry but have forgotten how, it's
been so long. Then when someone dies or the house burns
down, we feel an aching emptiness — as T. S. Eliot expressed it, "dry sterile thunder without rain." We speak
clinically of "processing" our emotions, analyzing our feelings and talking them through. But when deep emotions
are stirred there is catharsis and cleansing in the physical

flow of tears (and the momentary loss of control we so fear).

Maturing as adults may just mean learning how to cry again. I have a friend who says that when he needs to cry he listens to the right music alone in his car. Watching *cri de coeur* movies sometimes helps. A neighbor who lost her mother a few months ago was telling me she couldn't express her grief until someone suggested she write letters to her mother — as she always had. She had a good cry.

Once upon a time psychologists told us that all our emotional problems were caused by a failure to crawl in infancy. Remember that? If we skipped the crawling stage and went straight to walking, we had missed a crucial developmental period. And that would dog us throughout our whole lives. The answer was to get great big men and women on all fours. They had to go back and learn how to crawl.

I don't frankly believe in this bit of pop psychology. You don't need to crawl, but you do need to cry. There are moments in this crazy, cruel life when that is the only natural, healthy response. Children know instinctively how to do it. The rest of us have to practice until we reclaim the gift, for crying out loud.

Happily Never After

Are you happy?

I can't remember the last time someone asked me that question directly. As existential questions go, it may be less annoying than "Are you saved?" but it is still not the sort of thing we ask one another, or our own selves. It looms as a trick question. How exactly am I supposed to answer that? I just show up for work, take my meds, look after my stocks and my kids. I don't have time to navel gaze.

That simple question — Are you happy? — is considered either simplistic (everyone knows that contemporary life is too complicated for that) or threatening. Because that question begs the great big, elephant-in-the-middle-of-the-room question that no one is supposed to ask. Namely, now that you have, or are well on the way to having everything that is *supposed* to make you happy, are you?

I had lunch last week with a friend in the specialty food business, a career I thought he'd always been in. Turns out he started out in advertising. Madison Avenue. He got promoted, he told me, until finally he was made an account manager. To celebrate his success, his father came into New York and took him out on the town. "Over dinner," he said, "my father said to me, 'You don't look happy.'" And he wasn't. "In this ad business," he rued, "you're only as good as your last slogan." He didn't want to end up with a corner office and an empty life. What he really wanted was to start his own business — maybe a specialty food shop. Luckily, he had a father who encouraged him to take the risk.

The next day on his lunch hour he visited a famous food shop just to see about the possibility of a job. The manager wanted to hire him on the spot! In a moment of passion he took the leap. He went back to work and gave notice. On Friday he was back at the office, but on Saturday he was working as a weekend stock boy. Three weeks later he was full-time in an apron. "One day I was on Madison Avenue, eating in the best restaurants," he said, "and the next day I was a stock boy making five dollars an hour." But he was alive and excited again. In a couple of months he was working behind the cheese counter, trying to taste and master the subtle riches of a whole new world. Over the course of several years he learned every department, until finally he moved out of New York and opened his own shop.

Are you happy?

We ought to ask ourselves that question every day. Not, Are you doing the things that are *supposed* to make you happy (if not now then surely one day)? But, Are you happy now?

I find myself planning and working for the future, for payoffs and rewards in a month or a year, for which I am willing to pay with happiness now. Only to find of course that there is always another month, another year to wait. True, the future must be planned for, and there are surely rewards tomorrow for prudent action today. But somehow, I am learning, I must discover how to live a life of happiness today. Not someday when things quiet down and there's enough in the bank and I've gotten beyond these problems — but today. The idea that we can live temporarily unhappy lives in pursuit of payday/someday, when we will be set for life and ready for happiness, is a sad illusion.

Life is of a piece. The future is woven of the thread we spin today. It is silly to imagine that a "temporary" life of tension and stress is preparing us for a future day of relaxation and peace; that a provisional life spent compromising our ideals and deferring our deepest longings will one day give way to a future of fulfillment and deep joy. It doesn't work. "What shall it profit a man," Jesus asked, "if he gain the whole world and lose his own soul?" You can't live a soul-ebbing life and somehow pull out happiness in the end.

In a culture of achievement we naturally assume a path *to* happiness: get on it, do the work, and — enduring a baleful journey of indeterminate years — you will eventually arrive at bliss. But there is no path *to* happiness, only a path *of* happiness. In other words, happiness is a state, not a destination. You can't "get there" from here. It can only come to you. Wherever you are. Whatever your circumstances.

We live in a world where we are encouraged, in a cruelly ironic way, to work harder and longer for more and more that we cannot enjoy now. (Don't confuse this with the important discipline of deferring gratification, which is the fine art of allowing certain joys to mature and ripen like fruit on the vine, and which actually deepens both present and future happiness.) A little, inner alarm ought to go off when we hear ourselves rationalizing the present bleakness of our lives as the inevitable cost of a golden future — next year, or the year after that, or when we retire.

It doesn't work that way. I know too many people who tried to make the Faustian bargain — but only for a season. They put their soul, their happiness in temporary hock until they won the big prize, and they never quite got it back. And besides all this, there is that other little problem with the future: it's not guaranteed. We all know people who put all their happiness eggs in the basket of retirement, only to take sick the day they took the gold watch.

Are *you* happy?

Care of the Sole

Winter is hardest on shoes. I could wear galoshes but I don't, even though my mother always told me how hard water was on leather. Instead I slog through slush and half-jump salty puddles. So today I sit down to polish my shoes. I like doing this menial task.

I get the polishing kit and set up shop in the usual place, over an old rug that looks like it was already flecked and smudged with cordovan the day we bought it. I have three pairs of shoes, all looking scuffed and forlorn.

The old black pair I wear every day are the worst. I black out the scrapes and erase with a good rubbing the white stains on my right heel (it sits in a puddle under the car accelerator). Then I switch to brown for the casuals and finally to cordovan for the loafers I have had since Chicago days — going strong on sole number three. I give the little crevice between sole and upper a good going over with an old toothbrush loaded with polish. A seal against water . . . so hard on leather.

A man should be faithful to his shoes. So my father taught me when he called all the Anderson kids in on Saturday night. I don't know what the girls had to do, but the boys had to polish their shoes — that and do their Sunday school lesson. So I am still doing it, polishing both my shoes and my soul.

You don't throw away shoes. (My closet floor is full of old retired friends.) You wear them until they take the form of your crazy feet, and you keep them. I've got fallen arches and two bone spurs, and all my shoes have come to accept this. So I take care of them today, and it feels good. It's a simple act of faithfulness and care. It's sticking with something. It's seeing possibility in run-down things. It's the satisfaction we feel when we return from the hardware store with two dollars' worth of angle iron and screws that make an old sled fly again. We want to keep our promises to small things. In a world that always wants to know "what you make," we want to say it's what you keep and care for. In a world that insists on moving up to the next model, we want to say shinier isn't necessarily better.

I know this as I finally take the buffer to my dull friends. What comes up from the polished leather as I bear down on the brush is not exactly a shine — they're too old for that now — but a deep glow.

Caring about old things is a sign of age, I guess. Not many twenty-somethings go antiquing. When the shine of youth has left your face, you start looking deep, past the cracks and sags, for a glow. It's a richer, wizened beauty. But it's harder to see. Some never see it, in themselves or in others. A long time ago, in the silver vaults of London, an older friend taught a very young version of me how to tell sterling from plate. "It's sterling," said Craig, "when the silver seems to be lit from within."

So I keep polishing, looking for that glow, the light from within. In more than just shoe leather.

Stronger Medicine

One winter when most of America was sick, I spent two days in bed with a stack of unread magazines and the common cold. On the afternoon of the first day, when I was too miserable to read and unable to sleep, I began to miss my mother. My family had sympathized with me that morning as I slumped in my breakfast chair like a punch-drunk teddy bear, but no one wanted to get too close. Who could blame them? They went to school, to work, and left me to bed. I ached. I hacked. And still no one came to take my temperature.

Everyone knows, of course, that taking your own temperature avails nothing, whereas having your temperature taken is a glorious, healing balm. That's what my mother used to do. She would put me to bed and take charge of my life. Make me put on heavy pajamas and stay in bed! Then she would open her domestic arsenal and set upon my sickness. Out came the steam-puffing humidifier. She would sit on the edge of my bed and shake that thermometer with a wicked wrist, slip it under my tongue, and wait. Meanwhile, she took my temperature with a palm to my forehead, a hand to my cheek, in my armpit, on my chest. She administered a vile tablespoon of castor oil whether it was immediately called for or not, in the same way that a good mechanic, doing a tune-up, orders an oil change for good measure.

Then, if I had a cold or sore throat, she got out the Vicks VapoRub. She slathered the piquant salve on my chest and neck, and daubed it under my nose. Then she wrapped an old wool sock around my neck and secured it with a diaper pin. She gave me two aspirin, tucked me in, and told me to stay in bed! I lay there until I heard my father come home for lunch, and waited for him to climb the stairs and sit on the bed and check my temperature with the back of his hand.

Except for the aspirin, everything about my mother's doctoring seems shamanistic. My brothers and sisters still laugh incredulously when someone remembers that itchy wool sock. But it worked. We almost never saw the doctor (I remember only once when I did not get better and the doctor came to give me a booster shot), and yet all seven of us children recovered from every pediatric illness.

I thought about those corny home remedies while reading "The Placebo Prescription," a magazine article about the amazing effectiveness of placebos — the sugar pill with no medicine in it. Increasingly, clinical tests confirm that placebos work, sometimes as well as drugs, sometimes better. Even in surgery. In 1994, a respected surgeon named J. Bruce Moseley scheduled ten patients for arthroscopic knee surgery to relieve arthritis. But not everyone got the same treatment. Two got the standard procedure, the scraping and rinsing of the joint; three got the rinsing only; and five got nothing more than three scalpel stabs to simulate the scars of arthroscopy. How many reported feeling less pain after the procedure? All ten.

But the effectiveness of a placebo is not limited to the subjective feelings of a patient — "You know, I think I'm feeling a little less pain today." Some studies actually show physiological improvement after taking the "fake" pill or having the make-believe procedure.

Placebos work as well as they do, says author Margaret Talbot, because the "placebo effect" is larger than taking a pill. "It has to do with faith and hope," she writes, "and a physician's capacity for marshaling those sentiments in the service of the sick." People who don't get "real" medicine, the studies show, get well or feel better if someone spends some caring time with them, listens to them, and — this is sine qua non — touches them. "The availability of high-tech diagnostic tools," says Talbot, "and the shrinking of appointment slots means doctors are doing fewer physical exams even though the *laying on of hands* is perhaps the most basic source of human comfort" (emphasis mine).

"Laying on of hands"? I thought that was a church term. Those are in fact the ancient words of the liturgy for Ministration to the Sick: "Laying on of Hands and Anointing." Following Scripture and long tradition, we don't just pray for the sick, we touch them. We lay hands on them and smear sweet oil on their foreheads the way my mother used to anoint me with Vicks VapoRub. Which is exactly what it was: an anointing. I got better, I believe, not because of the curative properties of any of my mother's all-purpose tonics, but because someone made love palpable — and told me to stay in bed!

Those who understand the unity of human beings in body, mind, and spirit know there is a spiritual dimension to healing. The God of Israel promised to heal his people of every disease, and the Jesus of Christian devotion became the Great Physician. This healing tradition was not primarily about drugs, or even herbs, though it welcomed the standard doctoring of the day. It was grounded in the simple truth that sick people most need loving care. Whatever else we dispense, it averred, we had better give the sick liberal doses of encouragement and hope, and we had better touch them.

The best news in all this is that, when it comes to helping people who hurt, expertise is not the needful thing. Compassion is, and anyone can fill that prescription in spades. We all know people who need healing. Most of them suffer from things you'd never tell a doctor about, and most by far do not need any drug. They just need someone who will listen, lay a hand on a shoulder, understand, and listen some more.

If after that the symptoms persist, I recommend a wool sock.

The Cat at the Window

At summer's end I put up two bird feeders in our backyard. For a long time nothing flew in. Then we got a foot of snow and word got out that the Andersons had opened a kind of aviary soup kitchen. Boy, they came. We sat at the breakfast table in front of the big sliding glass door, eating our breakfast and watching the birds peck at theirs.

After the kids went off to school, I'd sit there with the newspaper and a fifth cup of coffee just watching them fight for a perch on the feeder. The big guys ate and the little guys waited their turn on the fence. One day, staring at the flurry of wings and the shower of sunflower shells falling black on the snow, I heard a little cry of pain. I looked down at the cat crouched beside the glass door. Oliver? That was no cat I'd heard. Like a soldier on his belly he was low on his hunting haunches. Then his body rose slightly and strained toward the glass as he let out a little cry, a whimper of anguish. Now I could see. It *was* Oliver. He wanted to do a cat's business with those birds.

A few days later I found myself watching Oliver again and not the birds. We were alone, the two of us on this side of the glass, and the boy in me sided with the cat. I know about trying to catch birds — and rabbits and little lizards. All the tantalizing prey of luckless boys. Oliver is just a regular house cat, but something in his sinews was still hardwired to hunt. All the birds within striking distance, though, were behind glass.

Very quietly then I went to the door. I slid it open. "Okay, boy," I whispered. Oliver slipped outside. The birds took one look and flew away, trailing ridiculous high-pitched laughter. It was cold and Oliver turned quickly back inside. I felt bad for him. He's not a very good hunter, feeding daily on Kibbles 'n Bits, but I knew what it was like to want to hunt. To want to go after something — something you feel born to pursue. To be behind a glass door looking out and afraid, really, that the door may open.

The Silent Dinner Bell

Everybody seems to have a theory about what's wrong with the American family. Mine can basically be expressed in two words: TV dinner. The idea that swept the United States in the sixties, that people ought to eat dinner in front of the television, led not only to bad food but bad families. Swanson's version of the evening meal quickly became a derisive byword: if you want to pronounce utter disapprobation upon a plate of food you can do no better than to call it a TV dinner. What has not come so quickly is the realization that bad food corrupts good relationships.

The pre-portioned meal-in-a-tin marked the end of eating family-style, where food is passed and shared and where people must talk to one another or fight or *something*. But once you trade a common dinner table — however simple the fare — for an individual TV tray, the family starts to separate about as badly as Mr. Swanson's creamed corn.

These days, the image of the American family gathering for dinner around the brand-new Philco is quaintly Rockwellian. Family dinner is way passé; we don't even sit together in front of the TV anymore. Hence my two-word theory. Once "TV" and "dinner" became associated, it was only a matter of time before the family became dissociated. We went from the dining room to the living room to everybody's got a TV in their own room. And everybody's foraging in the fridge for themselves.

I can hear the parents now. "Are you kidding? I can't get my kids to come home and sit down for family dinner." Maybe, maybe not. A recent YMCA survey of 200 young people, ages 12 to 15, and 200 parents of 12- to 15-year-olds, reports that "not having enough time together with their parents" is the top concern among teenagers today. In fact, teens are three times more likely than their parents to say that "not having enough time together" is their biggest issue of concern. What are the *parents* worried about? They're more concerned about outside threats, like drugs and alcohol, than they are about family time together. Among parents surveyed, quality time with the family comes in as the fourth most important priority.

In other words, parents, it's not the kids who don't want to spend time with you. According to the survey, "both teens and parents agree that parental work obligations are the number one reason why their family doesn't spend more time together." Parents today are legitimately concerned about drugs and alcohol, but, as always, the best defense against these and other outside threats is a strong relationship with your son or daughter. And for that, I believe, nothing compares with breaking bread together as a family. (Seems we need some work in that department, however. The YMCA survey found that about 30 percent of parents report having no more than four meals a week as a family, and 10 percent reported sharing one meal a week, or *never* eating with their teens.)

Maybe it's because I'm married to someone who cooks and writes about food for a living, but I believe it's well nigh impossible to overestimate the power of food — anything touched at least once by a human hand and offered in love. I don't know exactly why, but good things happen when people sit down and share a meal together. Whether we know it's happening or not, we are bound to the people with whom we sit at table. Even if Johnny rejects the vegetable du jour and Susie sulks. The food is still working its magic, nourishing body and soul of all who pass the potatoes, please, and help yourself.

If you're skeptical about the mysterious powers of family dinner, though, don't take my word for it. There's a recent study to prove it. This one by the President's Council of Economic Advisers, which found that "teenagers who had dinner with their parent or parents five nights a week were more likely than other teens to avoid smoking, drinking, violence and suicide." Now that we know our young people want to spend more time with their families, and knowing their legendary appetite — why not set the table tonight?

Oh, and one more thing. The best way to establish the habit of family dinner is to start early. The pastor of the first church Pam and I joined after we got married was a frequent dinner guest in our shag-carpeted little apartment. Like a lot of newlyweds, we started out with a card table in the dining room. The Reverend Craig Johnson surveyed the mostly empty abode (except of course for a boffo stereo) and said, "Well, I always tell newlyweds with no furniture to forget the waterbed and the living room sofa. First buy the finest dining room table you can afford, and everything else will take care of itself."

Amen. Let's eat.

The Stolen Sky

On a clear and blustery mid-October day I look through the yellow trees to see a perfect Magritte-blue sky. It is beautiful and it makes me sick to see it. It reminds me of the brilliant sky of September 11. Then it all flashes again: the plane, the sleek silver tower, the spectacular fireball billowing orange against surreal blue, the white plume of smoke drifting over the harbor. I can't stop the images — I watched them too many times that day and the day after and the day after. Now I wonder when I will be able to see so simple a thing as a beautiful blue sky and not look away. One day, I suppose. But for now they have stolen the sky.

We might say they have stolen our life. Or at least the dubious privilege of living it without too much thought. We cannot believe how two falling towers could knock down every pillar of American life like a line of dominoes. Now we've got to think hard about everything. If there are other "sleeper" terrorists living invisibly in suburbia, who can we trust? Are we free to travel? Will we end up with the thousands in the unemployment line? What about our investments, our future? The morning after disaster is supposed to offer the consolation that things can only get better. These days, we've got an inkling things could get worse.

Another plane may hit another tall building, but it's not enough to quit the big city and stay safe at home. Everybody's got mail. And the deadly anthrax sent to Congress and the media came from just down the road in Trenton, New Jersey. One day, walking back from the mailbox, I was riffling through a stack of letters. When I came upon a piece with no return address, I paused. I felt silly doing it, but I held the envelope up to the sun and shook it, listening for the soft settling of lethal powder grains. We are a nation on tenterhooks.

It is quite normal when one's life has been stolen to say, "I want my life back!" And the authorities are trying to oblige. We are roused with old slogans spitting in Fear's eye. We are bravely enjoined to come out of our craven hiding and take back our lives. How? By going back to the mall, of course. By taking the kids to Disney World. These presidential directives strike us as banal — even inappropriate, as a response to mass murder. But we all know he has to say it. An economy circling the drain has very real human consequences as well. And if the goal is to get our life back, to "get back to normal," it's the best thing we can do.

The only problem is, we are never going to recover our lost life. It's gone. We knew it and said so the day this all started. Acknowledging this is not defeatist or unpatriotic. It doesn't mean we take this heinous act sitting down and are willing to live under the constant threat of terror. No. We — and all people — deserve to live in peace and safety. And we will get there, but not by going back to the *status quo ante bellum.*

One thing I learned when our church burned down: the past cannot be recreated. When we lose a loved one, when we face debilitating illness, when we lose a career, a life's savings, a cherished dream, there's no going back. Any calamitous loss like this must be dealt with as a death. Mourn it, grieve it, have a good cry if you can. And then look east toward resurrection and new life.

In his autobiographical work, *A Whole New Life,* Reynolds Price recounts his mortal struggle with spinal cancer. Ten years after his diagnosis — years spent trying to recover his lost life — Price says it would have been far better if someone had walked up to his hospital bed on day one and said, "Reynolds Price is dead. Who will you be now?" His dramatic transformation begins when he gives up on the old dead self, and sets about the bracing task of discovering what new life God is calling him to live.

It is the same for all of us in America. We feel the feverish impulse to get everything back the way it used to be — to insist that the rest of the world either give us back our life or suffer our wrath. But all of that is dead. Who will we be now?

Anyone in search of a new life wishes it could be found complete, in one day. But here we walk by faith, not by sight. If we want to walk a new path, we have to take a single step in the best direction we know. If we want to live free from violence and terror, we must, in the words of St. Paul, "pursue the things that make for peace." And what makes for peace? Justice and equity. Let's take a step in *that* direction, understanding that we cannot live our lives, as the richest most powerful people in the world, without reference to the needs and dreams of all people. The world is just too small.

Mysteries —

Large and Small

⊚

Hearing Emily

Outside my office window lies a playground where our day school children race and tear and frolic at recess. I often catch myself staring at them for long moments, trying to remember when I, too, could play with unself-conscious abandon.

Blake Steffens was one of the boys who tore up that playground outside my window, until somehow he succumbed to the dread bacteria that causes meningitis. In a matter of hours the fire tore through his body and he was gone. At five years old.

The death of a child casts a strange spell on a community. We closed the day school and went into mourning. People I didn't know — who didn't know Blake — stopped me in the grocery store to ask how that boy's family was. A boy who dies is everybody's boy.

When I met with Blake's mother I felt helpless. I did not know how to plan or conduct a five-year-old's funeral, and I hope I never ever learn how. She brought pictures, a whole bag of photographs she had been gathering up, and for a time we simply looked at the pictures. We talked about the informal service she wanted to have just for all the day school children on Friday when school reopened, and about the funeral on Saturday. Between her sweet rememberings and sudden waves of grief, we managed to talk about music and readings and flowers.

On Friday we gathered all the day school children and their parents in the chapel. On this first day back after the tragedy, we needed to come together as a family for some songs and prayers. Some of the children sat in Dad or Mom's lap, as much for the parents' as for the children's sake. We talked about missing Blake, and then we sang "Jesus Loves Me." It felt funny singing that juvenile song again, but then I allowed myself simply to be as a child among children, and I sang like I was in Sunday school.

The next morning the church was filled, people stood in the aisles, for Blake's funeral. We read the Gospel story where Jesus took children in his arms and blessed them, we prayed the best prayers that would come from our mouths, and, at his mother's request, we sang Blake's favorite songs. He wasn't old enough to appreciate the old funeral standards like "Rock of Ages," so we sang "This Little Light of Mine" and "Jesus Loves Me."

This time it was mostly big people sitting out in those same oak pews. But I felt I was with the children again. This crushing pain, this numbing sadness flayed us and laid us bare. We felt like a tree stripped of its bark, down to its white flesh. We looked at that half-size white satin casket lying before the altar and felt scared and helpless as any child. Nobody felt funny singing "Jesus Loves Me" that day.

We walked behind the hearse as it slowly carried Blake's body from the church door to the cemetery at the top of the hill where we buried Blake. It was hard to leave the cemetery. People stayed a long time, mostly I think because it was cold in the January sun and we didn't want to leave the boy alone like that. It's always so final at the graveside. When everyone had gone, Blake's mother sat in one of the folding chairs set up under the tent. She watched as the casket was lowered, and said her last good-bye.

The death of a child is the worst pain a human being can endure. You look at the family and wonder how they can ever go on. You wonder if *you* ever could.

A death like that scares a community. All our adult pretensions to control and self-made security are stripped away, and we sit like children in shock. If this can happen — a child with eighty years to go can die in a matter of hours in a high-tech hospital surrounded by teams of medical experts — if this can happen, then everything is jeopardized. It can all be gone in a breath. We get up and leave for work every day as if the people we love are always going to be there when we get home. And that's not true.

For a moment we know Isaiah's cry, "All flesh is grass, and its beauty like the flower of the field. The grass withers, the flower fades. . . ." For a moment we can see how we ought to live, for what we ought to be spending our grassy lives. It doesn't matter what you make or what you drive or who thinks you're important. All of that is chaff and everybody knows it.

But only for that moment. And then the whole trauma fades like a passing train whistle and we resume our "normal" lives.

It's what Emily had to learn in Thornton Wilder's classic play, *Our Town*. She's the young woman who dies and goes up to join the others in the Grover's Corner cemetery. The newest arrival, she sits and talks with the others, people who now know the end from the beginning. "Why can't I go back to the land of the living?" she says. She wants to go back and relive her life, now that she understands it all. And no matter how they counsel her not to, she goes.

But no one among the living can hear her. "Oh, Mama," she vainly pleads, "just look at me one minute as though you really saw me. Let's look at one another." They're too busy with all the business of life. They can't hear Emily.

Sitting in the chapel, singing "Jesus Loves Me," watching dun earth fall on white satin — somehow then, Emily was getting through to us. For a moment we could hear her. We looked at each other one minute as though we really saw.

Hands Off: We Hatch Alone

Last week a box of chicks were hatching in the kindergarten classroom of our day school. There was a long line of children outside the class waiting to get a peek at the eggs. So I got in line. It had been a while for me, too.

As they moved through the line, all the children had their hands clasped behind their backs. I inquired why. Teacher's orders: This is how we approach mysteries that we cannot touch. Good idea. I put my hands behind my back, too. The eggs were small and quiet in the light. One was slightly cracked, another chipped, a small shell fragment lying below. But most were perfect and still.

We watched those eggs for the next week. When one hatched, the chick was moved into a box with the other free birds. But I kept noticing the quiet eggs, the few that couldn't seem to break free. In the kitchen with a cup of coffee I asked Annette, one of the teachers, what was wrong.

"Actually," she said, "we're doing pretty good. Odds are, 25 percent just don't hatch. And of course," she said, "you can't help them do it." Remember that childhood lesson?

It's worth remembering. We talk much about our interdependence, about helping one another, and it's true — to a point. But we cannot help a single other person hatch. If the task of life is to break continually out of the shells that confine us and into freedom, that is a solitary task. Helping doesn't help.

Every child must resist officious adults. "I want to do it *myself*!" The tendency of love is to do too much. We can't keep our hands off other people's struggling lives. We forget that the struggle is natural and necessary. It's painful and perilous to get to this world, and it's usually more of the same when we leave. No strife, no life. But every generation wants to spare its children the bitter struggles of its own enduring. What we now call the "greatest generation" often wonders how their children and grandchildren would have been able to endure war, Depression, rationing, universal sacrifice and hardship. The answer is simply that the "greatest" generation determined to eliminate for its children the very difficulties that made them great. They ran resistance for their kids, they gave them money for nothing and perks for free. They got them better jobs to start and acceded to the notion that they ought to have at the beginning of their lives everything their parents had at the end. And they did it absolutely in love.

Reinhold Niebuhr said, "I am never so dangerous as when I act in love." Not only romantic love is blind. Every so-called love that seeks to do for others what needs — crucially — to be done by oneself is blind to its own ego needs. When I seek to help others, what need is that meeting in me? Do I need to appear stronger? If my child fails, am I afraid of how that reflects on me, on my family? If we're not asking these questions, we're dangerous in love.

In twelve-step terminology, that kind of "love" is called

enabling. It's helping someone to death. Some of us have friends or family in that extreme plight. And all of us deal daily with ordinary people who need to hatch. Our job is to coach some and cheer for progress but mostly to leave them alone. Beautiful, life-giving neglect.

It was fun watching the chicks peck, wriggle, and kick their way into this life. But then I'm not a chicken. It's much harder when one of your own is on the dark side of that shell. Then it can hurt. Then it's life and death. Then we want to reach out and help . . . just a little. Our hearts actually get in the way; we forget that no one can break anyone else through.

Parents cannot do it for adolescent and adult children; husbands and wives cannot do it for one another; neither can friends. We cannot stop drinking for someone else; we cannot find someone a vocation; we cannot stop (or start) eating for another; we cannot lift the pall of depression or assuage the unspeakable pain of a single other person. If they are going to break into freedom, they will have to hatch themselves. We can keep the egg warm, and we must pray — but with hands folded behind our backs. For this is the only way we may approach mysteries that we cannot touch.

The Kiss of God

It is a chilly February Sunday and eight boys and girls are sitting with their parents and grandparents, aunts and uncles, in pews reserved at the front of the church. Today they are to receive First Holy Communion. They wear little red carnations on the finest clothes I have ever seen them wear. Little blue blazers, lace dresses, snap-on neckties and ribbons in their hair. We have prepared them for this day, and they are ready. Michael's mother tells me her six-year-old was up before dawn. Ready.

Before communion I invite all the children receiving First Communion to come and join me at the altar. We sit on the rug to talk. I ask the big question, "What will you do today that you haven't done before?" Their eager response tumbles out. We're finally going to give them the little white wafer and they're going to half climb the altar rail to get up high enough for a little sip of the funny-tasting wine. I can feel the energy. They're ready to take their place at the family table.

"But what," I say, "is *not* going to happen anymore?" They look at me puzzlingly. "What's not going to happen when you come with your family to the altar?"

Henry knows. "We're not going to get a blessing," he says.

Until now they've come with everyone else to the altar

rail, but for a blessing. One of my great joys is blessing the children. "The blessing of God Almighty, Father, Son and Holy Spirit," I say as I trace the sign of the cross on their foreheads, "bless, preserve and keep you, this day and always." But no more for these eight.

"I'm going to miss blessing you," I tell them, and they look at me like I'm a funny uncle. But it's true. I'm going to miss signing them with the powerful arms of the cross, holding each beautiful face in my hands as if they are my own sons and daughters. "Henry," I say, "I've been blessing you for six years." I can see he is eager to receive communion like the big people, but father-like, I am not quite ready for my own loss. Perhaps this is something of how a mother feels when a child is weaned.

I look over at five-year-old Will. A year ago his mother told me she went to kiss him good night. She lifted a tuft of hair and kissed him on the forehead. "Mom," he said, "that's where God kisses me every Sunday." She didn't know what he meant, she told me, until he explained. "You know, at church — at communion." When he kneels, and I reach down to bless him, I always lift the hair from his forehead and trace the sign of the cross with my thumb. And this, for Will, was nothing other than the kiss "of God Almighty, the Father, the Son and the Holy Spirit." I was dumb with awe. How could his little head imagine anything so impossibly beautiful and true? How could I have been the God-bearer in his drama and not even have known it?

"I know you'll now be holding out your hands to receive a greater blessing," I say to the eight children encircling me, "and I'm proud to see this day come for you all. But — just for me — would you mind it if we had the blessing one last time?" They smile and nod. A few giggle. Maybe they half want the blessing, but they don't want to disappoint me in front of everybody.

I move to the left and start with Amanda. She gazes up as I take her head in my hands. I look deep into the wide-open skies of her eyes as I trace the cross on her forehead. "The blessing of God Almighty," I begin to say, but my voice breaks slightly and catches in my throat. I finish the words in a whisper.

Then Nicole. Her dark hair is curled especially for today, and her hair ribbon matches her dress, as it always does. Her eyes sparkle with anticipation. I whisper my words and move on. Michael's white-blond hair is parted and plastered down with pomade. He is stiff as a board as I come to him. Henry — the redhead boy with a spirit to match, who calls out unsolicited responses to my sermons. And Lindsay who stands in a white lace dress, smiling as if she were about to become a princess. I crown her tender head with my hands and deliver myself of the Monarch's benison.

Children need blessing. They need the touch of utter approval, the look of complete affirmation. But not only little children. All of us are looking for that blessing. We have not ceased to be children, even as we grow into adulthood, and yet most of us have never received the blessing of our parents. Achievements and accolades, which must be earned, can never substitute for this absolute blessing. An acclaimed preacher once told me, "People come from miles to hear me speak, and yet when my parents come to visit, my father won't even walk fifty feet from the rectory to the church to listen to his own son."

Without knowing it, we long for our parents' blessing because it is the easiest way to know God's approval. (It is well known that a child's first God-image is tied to his or her own father and mother.) What we truly desire, then, is divine benediction. We want to know that in God's eyes we are affirmed. Even if we are estranged from mother and father — even if they were not particularly good parents and we have abandoned their world and rejected their values — still, we need their approval. We fantasize about a time when a mother or father would be able to touch us — a hand on our shoulder or upon our head — and say to us, "Whatever conflicts may have separated us, and whatever life you are called to lead, you will always be my son or daughter and you will always have my blessing."

But let's not hold our breath. Many parents cannot bless their adult children. I am not sure why, and the reasons are not particularly important. The good news is, it is possible to find that blessing elsewhere.

The best way to be blessed, of course, is to bless others. We can do this for our own children and grandchildren, and for all the children who live in our community. Teenagers need daily blessing as they struggle with issues of identity and worthiness. It is so easy to bless. Anyone can lay a hand on a shoulder and give the look that affirms, the touch that says without a word, "You are absolutely splendid to the core!"

As we reach out like this, it becomes easier to find

others — surrogate parents and grandparents, mentors, trusted friends — who are able in their own quiet ways to assure us of their own favor . . . and God's.

As I bless the children, I come to the end of the semi-circle. Will is the last in line. I pause slightly to size him up in his blue blazer, and he looks at his shoes. This is the boy who thinks I have the touch of God. And now whenever I come to bless him I can't help but feel strangely empowered. I become who he thinks I am. I know of course that it is not a good idea to pretend to divinity. On the other hand, why argue? If the only person in the world who can see clearly the God-ness within me is a five-year-old boy, I don't care. I'm not turning down the gift.

I take his head in my hands, and one last time my hand slides under the lock of hair falling across his forehead. My thumb cross-signs, my hands grip a little tighter, and I linger slightly over the last phrase, "this day and always." The final blessing is not only on Will. It is on me.

Letter to an Atheist

Dear Marcia,

It was just in passing — we were talking about something else when you mentioned that you didn't believe in God. I think you said something like, "I hope that's not a problem for you." I hope I can say now what I couldn't say at the moment.

First off, I like your honesty. There are way too many church people lip-syncing their faith, who would be better off — like you — just admitting their deepest doubts. Such seekers are, as Jesus put it to one questioning soul, "not far from the kingdom of God."

That said, I must tell you that "belief in God" — and whether we "do" or "don't" — is a nonstarter for the Almighty. God simply doesn't care about such things. Never has. That's our thing. We have reduced the knowledge and experience of God to a belief, which we either "do" or "don't." It's right in there with "Do you believe in less government . . . the death penalty . . . eating veal . . . ?" Some do, some don't. It's a free country. Next caller, please.

This is where we like to locate all the great issues of life; we want to make everything the province of our will. Including God. Do we or don't we "believe" in him. We want every last thing in the universe to come under the control of our will, our choice. (Psychologists call this ego, and theologians call it original sin. Same thing.)

I'm talking now about myself, Marcia. About my powerful need to bend the world to my will. I don't mean some evil, "selfish" motive. It's simply the assumption that I must set the agenda for my life. If I am to be happy and fulfilled as a human being, I must "make it happen." And of course this works ... for everything except love. The most important things cannot be willed. They can only be received as gifts.

God is love, says the Bible. I think we're alive on this good earth for one thing only — for love. Which is to say, for God. And this, Marcia, is not something we "believe in." Love is something we surrender to. It's about trust. Will we stop trying to wrestle the world into our hands and let life come to us? Will we stop pushing the river?

You don't have to apologize to me, a minister, for not believing in God. I, too, have stopped believing in God. That, I have found, is just one more thing for me to do. So yes, by all means, let's stop this believing business. Just long enough to surrender our hearts.

Yours,
David

Our Daily Meat Loaf

Every good story, said Aristotle, has a beginning, a middle, and an end. We know this is true, and yet we somehow believe that the story of our life is the one exception. It has a beginning, which we celebrate (at least initially) on our birthday, and a middle, which everyone bemoans at forty. But this story has no end. Theoretically, yes, there is the last page, "The End," death. But no one lives as if it will actually come to that.

The old dictum is *memento mori*, "remember death." And there isn't anything morbid about it. In fact, there is no joy or pleasure without the remembrance of death, because life has no meaning apart from its end. Imagine a basketball game without a clock, without the furious intensity of the last seconds and the shock of the final buzzer. The taste of October's first apple is a pleasure only because it is time-sensitive. No one cracking the skin of a Macintosh knows just how many Octobers remain.

Not long ago at a church supper a parishioner came over to me and said, "I want you to meet a friend." I could see a woman with white hair sitting over at her table. So we walked over and I shook the woman's hand and introduced myself. She said, "Oh, I've met you before. Do you remember?" I thought perhaps she had visited the church once, but I didn't remember. "No," I said, "I don't."

She said, "You witnessed the signing of my will." My eyebrows rose and I looked at her with more than a little puzzlement. She went on, "They told me I was dying, so I decided to revise my will right there in the hospital. When we needed somebody to witness my signature, my daughter went out in the hallway just as you walked by."

Now I remembered. I was walking through a hospital ward — it was about four years ago — and, just as she recounted, someone asked me to come into a room and witness the signing of a will, which I was happy to do.

Then the realization struck me. Here, four years later, was the dying woman! — eating her dinner and smiling at me in the pink of health. We stared at each other for a long moment, and then, quite flummoxed, I blurted, "You didn't die! Why didn't you die?" She said, "I don't know exactly. I was so sick — my life was slipping away and I didn't have the will to live anymore. And I wasn't eating. The nurses would plop down a tray but they knew I wouldn't eat it. But then one day," she said, "they brought me my favorite. Mashed potatoes and gravy and meatloaf. I ate a little of that. And I lay there and thought, 'I've got to eat to live.' Then no matter what they brought me I ate it, and it tasted good. I got my strength back and my will to live. I'm active now. I'm alive!"

We talked a bit more. She said she was a Catholic but had come to the dinner at our church with her friend, the parishioner who'd introduced us. I told her she was welcome anytime. Then I went back to my table, and in a moment I was caught up in the cross talk of dinner-table conversation.

But I went home thinking about that woman, the one I'd left for dead four years earlier. She was like a wraith, a spirit-being who had had one foot in Death's doorway and then backed out. What she said carried the weight of eternity. It was as if Lazarus himself had come to me and said, *Don't forget how good mashed potatoes and gravy and meatloaf taste. It's the heavenly banquet laid out before you every day.* In other words, *memento mori.* Remember death . . . and live!

It would be nice if you could simply live every day as if it were your last. But this isn't possible. You still have to show up for work. You still have to put the garbage out Tuesday night, on the half chance that Wednesday — garbage day — dawns anyway. We know only that life ends; *when* remains the mystery. Human life is thus defined: It is the beautiful life that is ending — someday. You can sit with a psychic, read the tea leaves, study the entrails or the Tarot cards, but you cannot know when. If we could, we would have the ultimate control we crave. But God mercifully withholds such knowledge, hoping we will choose humility and trust instead.

Remembering the end is radical relaxation: "our times are in His hands." We don't have to suck the proverbial marrow out of life every day (try sucking marrow every day of your life — it gets old). We don't have to grab and grasp at the riches of life, afraid they may be gone tomorrow. We can simply entrust our lives to the One who is the end of it all, the One who promises the gift of our daily bread.

That is what my dying friend discovered when the unwanted hospital tray was plopped in front of her, and the smell of mashed potatoes and gravy and meat loaf (even a hospital rendition!) awakened in her the desire to live today. Let's don't forget that.

Feel That?

Have you ever, in TV terms, been "touched by an angel"? Ever felt the touch of God? If I were asked such a question, my impulse would be to answer yes. Wired to a polygraph, however, I think I would have to say no, sadly. But I came close once. I came real close.

It happened one Sunday at the Healing Eucharist. We do this once a month, gather in the chapel for a meditative Eucharist at the late end of a Sunday afternoon. And I always stand in the sacristy — the clergy Green Room — and feel empty and perfectly useless.

Because I am ordained, I am the one to lay hands on those who come and kneel at the altar, anointing them with oil and praying for their healing. Others in the community are discerning whether or not God has also called them to join in this rite of health and blessing, but for now it is the clergy who have this privilege.

And privilege it is. It's just that I don't feel worthy of it. Here are all these people, I think as I put the stole around my neck — people who are living with sickness themselves, or are burdened for someone who is. I am not a healer. The Scriptures speak of a special charism of healing that rests on some gifted souls. But I do not count myself among them. All I have is this stole, the mark of my ordination, hanging around my neck like an ordinary green scarf. That and this vessel of healing oil.

The lay minister assisting at this service comes into the sacristy and we look at the clock. A sliver till four. Time to pray. I put my hand on Cliff's shoulder and close my eyes. In return I feel Cliff's hand on my shoulder. This is better. I am not going out there alone. I pause, the silence descends, the muscles in my shoulders relent slightly and I tell the Healing One what she already knows: the two guys holed up in the sacristy are not really very good at this. With respect and all, You had better get here fast. Amen.

About a dozen people are sitting in the congregation. In a moment I am standing among them reading the Gospel. A multitude is crowded around Jesus, Luke tells us. "They had come to hear him and to be healed of their diseases. And all in the crowd were trying to touch him, for power came out from him and healed all of them." Here were people touched by God. Literally. They could swear it and pass a polygraph. What about the rest of us?

The rest of us, listening to the old story, can only act out the parts. This story is all about touch, the power of touch. And so, one at a time, the people come forward and kneel at the altar rail. In a half-whisper I hear the request. Infirmities of the body, troubles of the mind, vacancies of the spirit. I dip my thumb in oil, cross-sign the forehead, wrap my hands around the crown of the head, and pray.

After several people have come to the altar a woman steps forward, and when she does, two or three others get out of their seats and follow her. Without a word or sign they know to come and stand with her and lay on a supporting hand. But a moment later, everyone is coming forward. A holy huddle forms. The people on the outside lean over the closer ones, and everyone presses upon her. I trace the cross of oil, reciting the three strong names of God. And when my hands touch her head, it is as if I am the one to be healed. In laying my hands on the kneeling one, I am touching — and being touched — by all. I know because I feel it.

When I was a boy we had an old freezer down in the basement that was improperly grounded: when you grabbed the handle, you got a slight electrical shock. It was a jolt if you weren't expecting it. But we used to go down to the basement — the neighbor kids, my cousins, anyone brave enough — and form a long line, holding hands. The one standing by the freezer would say, "Ready?" then touch the handle, as the shock rippled from hand to hand down the line. It was a cheap buzz.

I am only slightly embarrassed to report that the touch of the healing circle reminded me of that old freezer, and the long line of children amazed to discover that human beings are wired for conduction. It was, that night in the chapel, a quite powerful buzz.

A friend of mine, referring to his church family, always says, "I don't know if I believe in God, but I believe in the people of God." Me too. I don't know if I have ever been touched by God, but I know I've been touched by the people of God.

I'd take a polygraph on that.

Love on the Rocks

> For your servants love her very rubble,
> and are moved to pity even for her dust.
> *Psalm 102:14*

At about 10:45 P.M. on May 10 — Mother's Day — someone struck a match and destroyed Trinity Church. It is safe to say that nothing has been the same since.

The night our church burned I was plunged into deep shock. When I got there, the whole sky was lit up orange. Flames shot through the arched roof of the parish hall like a pyre. I parked next door. That far away, cinders were falling all around me. Firefighters appeared as helmeted silhouettes against the firelight. I don't remember saying or feeling anything. It all appeared at first as a fantastical, nightmarish scene. I had never seen this glorious old building immolating itself, and yet that was what my eyes were seeing. I half-stumbled around the building and found a clutch of parishioners huddled out front. We held hands and prayed. Then the fire chief moved us off the property. It wasn't safe.

There were nearly a hundred men from twenty-five companies there that night, armed with the crude, age-old weapons against fire — water and courage. The school and the parish hall were gone; our only hope was that the firefighters could save the church. But we watched as first the smoke and then the flames swept through and burst from the roof of the sanctuary. That's when I stopped comforting other weepers and began to wail myself. I spilled retching tears like a man with the dry heaves. *No, no, no,* I cried, like a little baby half-choking on its torrent of tears. My legs went to rubber and I shivered like a frozen man. When I could not cry any more, someone got a chair for me and I sat down.

In the days and months that followed, the vivid horror of that night gave way to a sort of pale, Sisyphean exercise. Everything was harder, like trying to write my own name left-handed. We worked out of the old rectory and worshiped across the street in a school gymnasium. All of our familiar patterns were broken. Long after the fire, I'd still get up and walk halfway across the room before realizing that whatever I was after had burned up months ago. Friends and neighbors supported us with steadfast love, and perfect strangers were unbelievably generous. But there were still days when I felt like a frontier missionary, when my work was about as basic as splitting logs to build a chapel, pausing only to dig a well and check my trap line for the night's dinner.

Three months after the fire, bulldozers crawled off flatbed trucks and made quick work of everything but the heavy stone walls of the 1876 church. When the demolition crew began piling up little hillocks of face stone, a friend who knew I was forever planning to build a deck off the back of our new home suggested I take a load of the salvage stone and build a terrace instead. I agreed. It would be a fitting memorial.

A week later, six tons of precious stones slid off a truck and into a pile in my backyard. The truck driver, who knew I was the callusless pastor, smiled and said, "Watch out you don't break your back, Reverend."

That evening after dinner I went out to look at my rock pile. The stones looked pinkish in the setting sunlight. They were scraped and scarred, and some were utterly black on one side. But I loved these stones. There in a microcosmic heap lay my church.

Though I didn't know it at the time, the truck driver was right. I hadn't even thought about getting the old mortar off these rocks. But the next day I began. I went into the garage and came out with a sledgehammer. Wham. One wallop and the ridge of mortar cracked. Another, and it fell clean away. This would be a cinch. I started a "clean" pile and went back for another.

After an hour or so the stones got bigger and heavier, the mortar tougher. I was staggering beneath one- and two-hundred-pound slabs. Even in the August shade it was hot. Stone after stone. Wham. Almost nothing. Heaving that weighty hammer, my upper body was weakening. I took a break, wiped my face with a gritty shirttail, and looked at the rock pile. What a foolish mistake. There was no way I could handle all this massive, unwieldy stone. And there was also no way I could get rid of it now. It was mine, and I would have to make a terrace or it would sit there forever like a cairn. I had no choice, really.

That pile of stones has come to bespeak, for me, the sheer doggedness of my life since the fire: the cold reality of daily coping sits like six tons of stone in my backyard. I cannot change this, though in my anger and frustration I weave in and out of denial and flight. If I didn't love this rubble, I would be free. But I do, and so I am not.

True enough, I didn't have to ask someone to dump these ruins in my backyard. But it doesn't really matter what I should have done, or how grief and hope made me naive enough to ask for tons of supposedly redeemable wreckage. I've learned not to play the what-if game. Life just is. One way or another we all end up with six tons of something in our lives. And though we pray instinctively for transportation ("Lord, get me out of this mess!"), growing a soul always means transformation. *Son of man*, so to speak, *can these stones live? Can they become, say, a beautiful terrace?*

And of course, along the way — slower always than the fervid pace of our prayer — we come to life, too.

But I am not there yet. To know the sequence of salvation is not to jump it. Right now my life, like those of so many of my brothers and sisters, is lying in a gloriously intractable little mountain. And my blinkered calling is to hit the rocks, in hope.

Providential Respiration

Pentecost is not a breeze.

Christians celebrate Pentecost (fifty days after Easter) as the coming of God's Holy Spirit. The story in the New Testament book of Acts tells how the downcast disciples of Jesus retreated into isolation after his death — and rumored resurrection — and that on the day of Pentecost the house where they were holed up was filled with a rushing wind, and that cloven tongues of fire rested on the heads of them all.

That's a madhouse scene. Wind and fire are a terrifying duet. But in the way that all the great, defining stories of our faith have been tamed, the storm of Pentecost has been downgraded to a breeze that barely musses your hair. It's worth remembering that as we consider this season of fire and wind — serious wind.

The blast that hit the house where the disciples had gathered on Pentecost blew in from the Beginning. The Pentecost story has the Genesis account of creation written all over it. After the Lord God sculpts man from the clay of earth, the first human being lies beautifully still, lifeless. And then God bends low and "breathes into his nostrils the breath of life." Only then does "man become a living being."

It is often noted that the Hebrew *ruwach* means both

"breath" and "wind" — it's all the same. Big deal. We speak of a person as being long-winded, a windbag, a blowhard. It's an old metaphor for breath. But what if it turns out that God's breath is capable of gale force?

This is the *ruwach* that rocks Pentecost. The same life-breath that inspired human beings at creation breathes life into the left-for-dead disciples. The new creation. But this is not a gentle zephyr. Listen. "And suddenly from heaven there came a sound like the rush of a violent wind." This is bring in the kiddies, close the shutters, tie down the patio furniture. It's violent. To be present at creation — and then the new creation — is to experience wild energy, awesome power.

Good thing, too. Because as we often pray, "we have no power in ourselves to help ourselves." If we have the breath of life it is because we have been in-spired. The whoosh of the Spirit has gusted in our lungs and we live and move.

The guide to daily prayer and meditation that lies on my lap every morning says, "This air that you are breathing in is charged with the power and the presence of God." I am coached to breathe in God with every inhalation. Sometimes I am able to take in God like this and rest in the ocean of divine oxygen. Other times my chest is weighed down with anxiety or sorrow and my breathing is shallow, my heart is churning. Physically, spiritually, I can hardly catch my breath. If this depends on me, I choke. The wind from above must blow.

Several years ago I was called to our local hospital. I am an on-call chaplain and this was my night. My beeper went off and I called the hospital. The nurse said, "We've got a little child coming in — possibly DOA — come as quick as you can." When I got to the hospital I found that it was an eleven-month-old boy who had drowned in the bathtub. How it all happened was a blur, but he was quickly found and the paramedics had done CPR and artificial respiration.

When I saw the child in the emergency room, the staff had gotten his heart beating, but he was not breathing on his own. The nurse at his head, surrounded by six or seven frantic workers, had a mask over his nose and mouth and was squeezing the oxygen bag, breathing for him. When one arm tired of the squeezing, she switched to the other arm, and then someone took over for her. They kept pumping and pumping breath into his lungs.

Very soon the doctors decided to transfer the infant to a children's hospital in Philadelphia, because they would have a respirator for a boy his size. One of the doctors explained the crisis. There was water in his lungs, so the air had to be forced in. And the respirator could do that — force rich oxygen down his windpipe, fight against the water and push the lifesaving air into his lungs.

I met in a side room with the mother and father of this little boy. Of course they were devastated. But the first thing they asked me to do was to baptize their son. The hospital staff had told us that his hopes for survival were not good, and his parents wanted him baptized — tonight.

When the winded ER crew had stabilized the child, the doctors and nurses opened a little pocket for us near his head. With his mother and father I stood while the nurse drove oxygen deep into the infant's lungs, and with a Styrofoam coffee cup hastily filled with tap water, I baptized the child in the name of the Father and of the Son and of the Holy Spirit.

The memory of that nurse, squeezing that oxygen bag over and again, is a God-image for me. It is so like Yahweh, on hands and knees, breathing powerfully into our nostrils the breath of life, blowing with the violent force of Pentecostal *ruwach*. Because we are all lying on that ER table. We cannot breathe on our own, and it's not enough to have one magic breath puffed into body and soul. If we are to live, God is going to have to get down on hands and knees again and work hard, pushing spirit and life deep within. We are drowning in our own fears, our lungs full of all the stuff we swim in.

After the baptism *in extremis* I left the hospital as the child was prepared for transfer. A few days later I called the children's hospital, and the nurse on duty told me they had taken the boy off the respirator. He was breathing on his own now — and sucking a bottle, too.

A Little Child Shall Drag Them

When we lost our church to fire, Trinity Day School was homeless — with a month left of school to go. Our good Quaker friends down the road immediately offered us their education building, which wasn't being used on weekdays. Seven long days after the fire, school reopened at the Solebury Friends Meeting House.

I was one of the adults called in to be with the children after the trauma, to assure them that things were going to be okay as everyone moved into a brand new place.

It was like the first day of summer camp on the pastoral and peaceful grounds of the oldest house of worship in Solebury township. Sun filtered through the great maples and turned green patches of grass yellow-white in the breeze. Quiver Farm, a petting zoo on wheels, had been called in to help make the day as warm and fuzzy as we could make it for these little ones. The lawn was spread out with a goat, a calf, a little lamb, a turkey, lots of ducks, baby chicks, rabbits, and a puppy-size piglet that looked (and squealed) like the porcine star of *Babe*. The old stone Meeting House looked down on this peaceable kingdom of children and creatures with a silent blessing.

I stood, taking it all in, until I felt someone rapping on my leg as if it were the front door. It was my friend, Olivia. She had come knocking the morning after the fire, too.

Standing in a drizzle, watching the rubble smolder and smoke, I had looked down to find her tugging at my pocket. I knelt down for a hug. Maybe she could see that I had been up all night fighting the fire with helpless tears because she offered up a faint smile.

Now a week later she was back and we were standing in the sun. She was wearing a pink summer dress straight out of the box. I said, "I like your new dress." She said, "I got it at Toys R Us — I mean, Kids R Us." Then she grabbed my hand and said, "Let's go see the playground!" I was thinking about it when the race car in a pink dress took off with my hand attached to the bumper. I was running. *In my suit* I was running. Then she let go. "Try and catch me!" she called over her shoulder, and punched it. Now I was really sprinting. My pen flew out of my pocket. I felt exhilarated and a little embarrassed. But that passed in a moment. Then I just felt good. For the first time since the trauma I forgot about it — for nearly twenty still seconds. Every other moment, waking or sleeping, I smelled smoke and saw flames erupting like a volcano from the rocky slate peak of the sanctuary I loved. But now, running after Olivia, all of that receded and I was free to experience the simplest joy.

Even twenty seconds in a place where we are free (which is another way of describing love) can heal a wounded heart. But often we can't get to that place by trying. We have to be pulled through the door. This is grace, when an unwitting child pulls me into twenty seconds of fire-forgetting joy. Grace is the mysterious pull from somewhere beyond my own little self. Only later, catching my breath, do I realize that I have been to another place and back.

Olivia drags me to pet a yellow puffball of a chick, then impetuously she dashes for the ducks, then the rabbits. I want to stop for the goat, but she isn't interested and makes a beeline for Babe.

Soon it is time to go, by classes, into their new rooms. Inside, the children survey the playscape. A boy named Chase eyes a box of blocks and drags it to the center of the room. Cody joins the building project and I ask if I can play too. I get down on the carpet.

A tower begins to rise. Cody uses a Tonka bulldozer to push massive blocks, ten-ton pillars, and curved arches toward me. My fingers become a heavy crane lifting the blocks into place until we have built a city with four gates and a tower in the center. Chase takes two flat red blocks and tells us he is building a fire next to the tower. I stop cold. "A fire?" I say. "It's in a fireplace," he says without interrupting construction. Then I know that Chase is just like me. He is always thinking about the fire, too. But like most children his fears get played out — literally. This is healthy and good. We're managing the fire: it's in the fireplace. So we keep building the tower until, of course, it is so high that the boys cannot help but accidentally tip it over. *Sic transit Gloria mundi.*

We end the morning out under the maples again. The animals have all been crated up and carted off. We sit on the grass and sing, "Will the Circle Be Unbroken?" and "The Lord's Been Good to Me." Psychologists talk about "reversion" in times of crisis and trauma: a child will start sucking his thumb again, an adult may go back to smoking. I feel in reversion, sitting with these children and singing my thanks for "the sun and the rain and apple seed" and feeling very good, actually.

Maybe when everything burns down around you it's all right to revert. To let yourself get pulled into the playground, to build an imaginary city out of the ashes, to sing the simplest songs again. I don't know if it's right, but it feels true.

Prayer Mail

Dear Jesus,

I tried praying today and you weren't there again. So I decided to write you a letter. I've always been better at letter writing.

I know you won't take offense, but sometimes you're a hard man to find. The other day a woman whose son is sick in the hospital told me she keeps praying the same prayer and it's getting her nowhere. Since I am a pastor I did the right thing and told her to keep on praying. I should have told her to write you a letter. I know she writes a mean postcard.

What can I tell you? I feel like I should ask you for something or confess something, sort of get the ball rolling here. But I don't tend to do that in letters. I just talk about my life and so on. So let's just start with today. Feel free to jump in whenever.

Last night a heavy storm brought down a blanket of branches and green oak leaves, and I had to clean up the lawn. Since the roads were closed, the kids were home from school today and Maggie and Sharon had no excuse not to help me. I got us three rakes from the leaky tool-shed. Then we fanned out across the backyard, peeled back the loose leafy layer from the grass, and whipped it like a wave that rolled down the lawn. It was almost fun, at first. The wind after the storm gusted clean and cool, and the September sun cut on a slant through the trees and made them yellow-green again like spring. I stooped to pick up a leaf pile and, I swear, fifty green acorns tumbled out like soft little golf balls. I put down the rake and scooped them up with both hands and threw them into my new yard cart with the giant orange sticker on the side still begging $39.99. It felt good. Our arms got tired after an hour and a half, and we bickered the last thirty minutes. But I'll take that ratio of blessing to bane any day. Thank you.

Of course I paid for all that bending and heaving with my back. I came in and took three Advil. You know about my back, I guess. But every time it goes I feel old and irreversibly damaged. Which reminds me of the beard I grew this summer on vacation. Heavily gray. I have not worn a beard in fifteen years and I was a little dismayed. Actually, I was secretly embarrassed that I was as dismayed as I was. I wonder if you can understand this. It is certainly true, I know from Bible and creed, that despite your divinity you are fully human and experienced everything that we mortals celebrate and endure. But you did not have to grow old. You lived only the first half of life, and you thought the world was ending in your day. I am doing the best I can as I slip into middle age and the world sputters into the third millennium of our Lord.

Anyway, after I took the Advil I just sat around because it was my day off. Then I read a book, actually about the quest for the historical Jesus. I look at my shelves and I suppose I've read two hundred books about you. Seems like I ought to know you better, really. Jump in here if you feel so inclined. . . .

When dinnertime came, both of my vegetarian girls were gone for the night so Pam and I decided to have a steak. I like how she turns the cast iron skillet on low for about twenty minutes just to get the thing superheated. And when the rib eye hits the pan I turn the exhaust fan on high but the smoke alarm goes off anyway. I honestly think she believes it's not a good sear if the smoke alarm doesn't go off. We had just that and a salad with blue cheese and the Cabernet that George gave us, which tasted very good for being free. And I would say that that was almost as good as the green wave of leaves this morning, and the clean gusts of rain-washed wind and all the acorns.

Not much else. The girls came in late but on time. Their night, however, is far from over, since they rented a movie on the way home. They will stay up now until two, and in the morning we will find diet Coke cans and dirty dishes and an empty Oreo box on the coffee table even though they are supposed to clean up. But we are going to bed. I will try you again in the morning and if I can't get through I will definitely write.

> *Yours, I trust,*
> *David Anderson*

Slowing to a Fast

Years ago someone told me that brown rice and papaya was a proven "cleansing diet." If I ate nothing but brown rice and papaya for three days, and drank nothing but green tea, my system would be cleansed and purged of all the chemicals and poisons that taint the food chain these days.

I remembered this odd regimen about a week after Thanksgiving. Holiday feasting had lured me into bizarre eating patterns, and I had fallen off the exercise wagon. After all the feasting I decided it was time for fasting. The two go together. In fact, the Christian year is a cycle of feasts followed by fasts, leading through the pangs of hunger to the feast once more. If I didn't fast now, I reasoned with myself, I could not enjoy the coming Feast of the Incarnation (that would be Christmas).

I start this diet by doing the most important thing: I find another sucker to go on it with me. My wife.

We begin on a Monday morning. I find a little brown rice in the pantry and boil it for breakfast. Supposing that papaya will be hard to find in these winter climes, we cut up whatever fruit lies in the basket. And finding no green tea (luckily), we steep whatever decaffeinated leaves we can find. Except for the odd combination of foods, it is not all that bad. What a lovely sort of discipline, I am thinking at the breakfast table.

At the lunch table I am thinking, Isn't this what I had for breakfast? And at the dinner table I am just thinking, This is not right. My children are eating pasta with red sauce and mocking their parents' fare. A glass of anything would at least be a distraction, but alcohol is verboten. The tea tastes bitter. I go to bed early.

On day two I awake feeling empty but okay. I wander downstairs, take my morning vitamins, and start scooping coffee into the machine like a robot. I pour the coffee back into the can and put water on to boil. Yesterday I was resistant. Today I am resigned. Hardly hungry. Coffee stimulates my appetite. Just the smell of it. Take away my coffee, give me bitter tea and reheated brown rice, and I would rather eat nothing. Which is what I eat with the morning paper.

When I sit for prayer and meditation, though, it feels good to be empty. I close my eyes and take a deep belly breath. Empty inner space. Space I am quick to fill. Thoughtlessly, like a robot, I fill it. There is a kind of satiety that comes with denial. I know this feeling from other fasts. I feel stronger than my hungers, more powerful than food. My light burns cleaner, my mind brighter.

I knew a girl in high school who fasted the week before final exams. She said it increased her brain power; the rest of us thought she was brilliant but crazy. Hunger would surely distract a fasting student. Actually, Jeanne Bowley was just too far above us in those days. Our adolescent bodies racked with hungers galore, we could not imagine what happens when the pangs lost their power over us.

But my meditation high does not last. By ten o'clock I am sitting in the staff meeting staring at the coffee. I have a slight headache, a caffeine craving, I presume. I pass the pastries without helping myself. I am not so much hungry as lost. I have an office routine, and I am not in it. Like a smoker, I need the thoughtless cup of coffee in my hand to do business. I need the pastry not simply for the sugar burst but to be a part of the group. I don't like explaining my abstinence.

On day three I have given up on the brown rice completely. It tastes like wet sawdust. I have bought some tea I almost like, and I sip that with fruit. I have passed the hunger point and boredom has set in. Mealtimes are no fun. Half the joy of everyday eating is preparing to eat, asking What shall we have?, eating a few olives while cutting up a salad, choosing a wine, talking about anything, maybe putting on some music. At five-thirty I fantasize about the richest, most intense flavors in my taste memory: pasta alla puttanesca, gorgonzola, osso buco. And yet it is only deprivation that drives me to concentrate and savor these flavors on my mind's palate. In fact, when I eat these dishes, I do not savor them, not nearly so intensely as when they are taken from me.

This is the wisdom of the fast. I remember a friend from Chicago days, Rick Lobs, who went on a Lenten fast. At Easter he reported an almost illicit taste sensation at the Eucharist. How rich and sensuous the little scrap of bread, the little drop of red wine on his tongue. It tasted, he said, like a feast.

At the end of the three days, I loathe brown rice so utterly that I swear I will never do this again. But I will. Not now, though. This is the greatest feasting season of the year — twelve days of Christmas, followed by New Year's on the secular calendar, and the feast of the Epiphany in the Christian cycle. But one cold day in February when the ash hits my forehead and I have forgotten how heavenly osso buco tastes in my imagination, and how empty inner space feels when I sit for prayer, then it will be time to fast. And brown rice will take me there.

The Christmas Visitor

Like you, I do not "believe" in Christmas.

Christmas in America is just like a trip to Disney World. We are thrilled to see our children taken in by the land of make-believe while they are still innocent enough to believe. That a Magic Kingdom really exists here on earth. That enchanted castles rise off the pages of story-books. That real cartoon characters walk the streets. That everything is free! Through our children we recall and re-live our own innocence, but of course we do not believe.

I have always thought it odd that newlyweds should honeymoon at Disney World, or that retirees should vacation in this kiddy paradise. But we all long to believe, to be in a place where, in the willing suspension of disbelief, we can stroll the immaculate streets of a magic kingdom.

Like Disney World, Christmas is a conjured experience we are called to believe in. And once we realize that the "magic of Christmas" is an elaborate domestic and capital-ist production, we join the ranks of the Christmas work-ers — the ones who make Christmas happen for the in-nocent.

Now, I know what you're thinking: the church is sup-posed to be the one place where we hold out for the true meaning of Christmas. Every year we make a faint effort to call people into the spiritual mysteries of the season, but by late November the only mystery on everybody's mind is, How are we going to pay for all this?

It's hard not to be a Yuletide cynic. I'm not a scrooge. I loved making paper chain to festoon the living room when my kids were young — I like to make Christmas happen for other people. But when that's your job, it's hard to make any room for Christmas yourself.

As a parish pastor my main job is making Christmas happen. That's all I do for the month of December. The first Saturday in December we orchestrate a tour of lavishly decorated houses and a Christmas Shoppe that rivals the aisles of Wal-Mart. From there it's on to Lessons and Carols, the choir's annual *Messiah* concert, the staff and volunteer Christmas luncheon, to say nothing of the sacred drama that puts overstimulated, sugar-addled children in bathrobes and sheep's clothing for the videographic delight of their parents and grandparents. When we've recovered from the Christmas Pageant, there is still communion to take to all the parish shut-ins, Christmas Eve liturgies to plan. And one more thing. I am expected to find the creative leisure to write and then deliver a sermon that, well, makes you believe in Christmas. And it'd better be good: for half the congregation it's the only sermon they'll hear until *next* Christmas.

It was December 22. I was sitting at my desk proofing a service bulletin when a call came in. The receptionist said someone wanted to talk to "the pastor." That means either someone wants to sell me something or someone wants assistance — they want money.

This bulletin was past deadline, I had two home communion calls to make, and I hadn't even started my sermon. I was not keen on taking this call. But I picked up the phone, put just a shaving of ice in my voice, and introduced myself. It was someone wanting assistance.

The story came pouring out. He and his wife had come up from Florida to visit a sick relative — he'd taken time off from work. But then their car had broken down, and they'd spent all their money getting it fixed. A church had put them up for the night in a motel, and some food pantry had given them a meal. But it was checkout time at the motel, and the car was fixed and ready to go. He said they wanted to make it home for Christmas.

But they needed, he figured, two and a half tanks of gas (besides the full tank they were starting with). He and his wife would trade off driving, he said, and make the twenty-two-hour trip nonstop. But they had to have gas.

He said he wasn't a slacker. He said he was humiliated to beg. He said I could call all kinds of people to verify the truth of his story. Of course that's what they all say.

I didn't know if I believed him, but it didn't really matter. Several parishioners had given me gifts and asked me to use the money to meet special needs like this over the holidays. I figured this must be it. Besides, I wanted to take care of this so I could get back to making Christmas happen.

So I said, "Let's get you some gas money, and I don't think you ought to drive all night. You don't sound like you're twenty-one and I know *I* can't pull driving marathons like that anymore. So let's get you enough for a good night's sleep and a couple of hot meals for you and your wife."

He was thrilled. In a minute I gave him directions to the church so he could drop by and pick up the money. He thanked me again. Then just as I was about to hang up I said, "Wait, I didn't get your name." I was about to meet this guy and I didn't even know what to say when he walked in and I shook his hand.

He said, "Joseph — Joseph Visucci."

I said, "All right, Joseph. And your wife?"

He said, "Mary."

I paused. Was he kidding me? I almost said, "By any chance — your wife wouldn't be expecting a child, would she?"

"I'll see you in about an hour," he said, and hung up.

These are the wild stories I always share with people in the office. It's church watercooler stuff — we've heard every scam in the book. But I sat on this one. I couldn't tell anyone this story because — my silence was telling me — I believed this man. I believed his story. I believed his name, and his wife's.

Was it just a coincidence that, as I was trying to manage Christmas and make it "happen," I should get a call from a man named Joseph, with a wife named Mary, trying to get back to their hometown? "Coincidence," the saying goes, "is God's way of remaining anonymous." How do you decide what is hokey and what is holy? Am I so afraid of seeming like the people who see Jesus in a taco shell or Mary in the whorls of a tree stump that I cannot give myself to an unvetted encounter with the supernatural? St. Teresa of Avila said, "The important thing is not to think much but to love much." Am I thinking too much?

I sat in my office, still trying to decide this case. Finally it occurred to me: What am I waiting for? If I have been interrupted in my somewhat cynical Christmas chores by a real Joseph and Mary on a journey to their homeland, and I refuse to believe that God is at least winking at me, then what am I waiting for? What would it take for me to believe? Joseph and Mary in full Sunday school pageant regalia riding a donkey into my office?

On the way to the bank to get some assistance for my Holy Family, I thought, This is my moment. Angels have come to my doorstep, and this Christmas I have the astonishing privilege of giving aid to the Mother of my Lord and his gentle but strong Protector. But on the way home I felt like a fool. Some hard-luck drifters had hit me for cash and I was trying to make them into angelic visitors. If I told anybody what I sensed might be happening here, they'd laugh.

So let them laugh. Finding God in the ordinary is a way of seeing the world. It's a willingness to suspect God when no other fingerprints match. When we encounter the sublime, terrible, inexplicable, we can stop silent in our tracks and whisper the words of Jacob as he awoke from his ladder dream: "Surely the Lord was in this place and I did not know it." Or we can shrug it off as weird coincidence.

We are hungry for the Spirit, desperate to enter the spiritual realm and know — please! — that there's something more than this visible world, what the poet Robert Bly calls the "doggy world." But we are looking for some idealized, angels-with-real-wings experience, some Disney World or childhood Christmas memory, so that when God accosts us — as God always does — in the scuffed imperfect world of our real experience, we walk by as if blind. We can't see that the world right in front of us is teeming with the divine life of the One who came among us as flesh of our flesh and bone of our bone. We can't make the leap from Sunday school religion to the actual lives we live. We are embarrassed to name our own experience as transcendent.

When we have lost our faith in the magic of Christmas we are finally ready to receive the truth. The meaning of Christmas is: God has visited us. In a tiny infant, the life of God is lived out in human life. So then, if you want to know God, know human life. And start with your own. God is beckoning us, wooing us, leaving calling cards all over the place — if we will to see. What are we waiting for? What would it take?

When I had finally met Joseph he did not have a lovely beard or any other sign of preternatural presence. He was just a gracious man in a hurry. Mary was waiting in the car. We talked for a minute and he left.

I sat down at my desk. If I somehow believed in this event, what did it mean? I was thinking too much again. I went back to my Christmas preparation and tried to be like the woman waiting in the car, the one who sat by a manger with a welter of questions and simply "kept all these things and pondered them in her heart."

Acknowledgments

Thank you to Mollie Hallowell, editor of *Trinity Tidings*, with whom I am privileged to serve; to Barbara Ogilby-Hames, who invited me to write for the *Pennsylvania Episcopalian;* to the Lilly Endowment, which funded the sabbatical during which this book was finally finished; to Sarah Jane Freymann, who first read my stories and persevered until we found a publisher; to my editor, Joanne Wyckoff, who gave shape to a formless collection of stories and breathed life into this project; to David Coen, the copy editor, who seemed to know just what I was *trying* to say, and showed me how to say it; to my brother, Michael Anderson, who has been reading my stuff faithfully and critically for twenty-five years (counting the awful poems and stories I wrote in college); to Jerry Rardin, who teaches me how to sit at the edge of the unknown; to the people of Trinity Church, with whom I have lived the best ten years of my life; and finally, to my daughters, Margaret and Sharon, who always granted permission to tell the stories they showed up in; and to my wife, Pam, a seasoned author who is my first and most trusted editor, as well as my friend for life.